DIANE LINCOLN

SCIENCE DISCOVERY FILES

10 FORGOTTEN STORIES OF INCREDIBLE SCIENTISTS

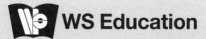
WS Education

NEW JERSEY · LONDON · SINGAPORE · BEIJING · SHANGHAI · HONG KONG · TAIPEI · CHENNAI · TOKYO

Published by
WS Education, an imprint of
World Scientific Publishing Co. Pte. Ltd.
5 Toh Tuck Link, Singapore 596224

USA office: 27 Warren Street, Suite 401-402, Hackensack, NJ 07601
UK office: 57 Shelton Street, Covent Garden, London WC2H 9HE

British Library Cataloguing-in-Publication Data
A catalogue record for this book is available from the British Library.

SCIENCE DISCOVERY FILES
10 Forgotten Stories of Incredible Scientists

ISBN 978-981-124-357-8 (hardcover)
ISBN 978-981-124-402-5 (paperback)
ISBN 978-981-124-365-3 (ebook for institutions)
ISBN 978-981-124-367-7 (ebook for individuals)

Illustrator: Diane Lincoln
Desk Editor: Daniele Lee
Design by: Eliz Ong

Printed in Singapore

Images used under license from Shutterstock.com: Pages 9, 10-11, 12, 13, 14, 19, 22-23, 26-27, 32, 34, 38, 42, 43, 44, 49, 55, 60, 64, 74, 76, 98, 103 and 112-113

CONTENTS

FOREWORD

As a former science teacher, some of my fondest classroom memories are of story times. Yes, we had story time in my science class!

I always believed that reading was important, but when I asked my teenaged students to find science books in the library, I was surprised to learn just how few books existed for that age group. There were reference books and biographies, but interesting accounts of how scientists made their discoveries were hard to find. Luckily, being an avid reader and a lifelong science enthusiast, I had learned many interesting tales about scientists. I decided that if the students could not find the stories to read themselves, I could at least share my anecdotes about how we learned what we know, and tell them about the people who made it possible.

There was an empty file folder on my desk that I would occasionally open and pretend to read from. All of the stories I told using this prop would be about whatever science topic we were currently studying. When I finished telling the tale, I would challenge the students to research it on their own and report back on any details I might have missed. They were always amazed that my invisible stories were real.

I don't remember the first time I used this technique to motivate science-learning in my classroom, but eventually the students themselves began to request story time. They would often ask to hear about a scientist that was like them in some way. When they asked, "How do we know that?", they were happy to see me reach for my empty folder to explain.

Science Discovery Files is a written compilation of some of the true stories from my imaginary book. I'd like to see a day when many similar books telling tales of exciting science are available in libraries for young adults, like my students, to read. I hope that as you read this book, you learn about the real science behind these stories and are inspired by the amazing people in these tales. But most of all, I hope you enjoy reading these accounts as much as my students enjoyed hearing them.

Walter Alverez and his father, Luis, near an exposed portion of the K-Pg Boundary.

CHAPTER 1

Solving a Mystery with His Father

- Walter Alvarez

One day in the early 1960s, a college student named Walter Alvarez eagerly examined rock samples with a magnifying glass. There were rocks made from lava and others made from sand. It wasn't the rocks themselves he liked. He was interested in what they could reveal about Earth's history. He didn't know it at the time, but someday, by studying rocks, Walter would answer a question about Earth's history that had puzzled scientists for over a hundred years.

Learning about rocks had come naturally to Walter. He and his sister would go rock hunting, near their California home, with their mother when he was younger. It made sense to Walter that rocks containing fossils were formed when seashells or remains of animals got covered with dirt and sand. Over millions of years, the shells or bones became buried deep in the ground. He could imagine how the lower layers got pressed really hard under the weight of all the earth above, squeezing the particles into rock. Walter understood that rock builds one layer on top of the next, so older fossils would be found in the deeper layers.

Walter was inspired by the thought of piecing Earth's history together using clues left in the rock. He called it "reading the story in the rocks." He became especially excited when he was taught how mountains are formed. He learned that a series of repeated earthquakes can slowly, over millennia, crack the ground and push large areas upward to form mountains. The ancient rock layers then become exposed in mountain canyons. Walter couldn't wait to investigate these visible rock layers in the mountains.

After graduating and working for a few years, Walter took a research position at Columbia University in New York City. He wanted to uncover the history of the Italian peninsula. At

A modern student studying rocks the same way Walter Alvarez did.

Columbia, he learned about magnetic changes in rocks. These changes would support a new idea that scientists were attempting to verify. He was learning a great deal, but there were some very curious things that Walter was yet to discover when he went to Gubbio, Italy.

The town of Gubbio existed before the time of the Romans. Narrow streets wind past white stone walls, arches, and towers.

In this image, the K-Pg Boundary has been bent by dynamic Earth forces.

Ancient stone bridges cross a meandering stream that runs through the town. Here, Walter admired statues and tossed an occasional coin into a fountain. He climbed streets built long ago as staircases for horses. Walter could see the Apennine

66 Ma

Paleogene | **Cretaceous**

Mountains, visible from every Gubbio street. These pink limestone mountains were the reason he had travelled to Italy. They held many uplifted rock layers that could be sampled for magnetic changes.

These are common tools used by geologists; the things Walter Alvarez carried with him.

The knapsack that Walter carried with him to explore mountains held a notebook, pens, a little hammer, a chisel, and small plastic baggies. There was also a compass, a magnifying glass, a ruler, and of course, a canteen of water and a snack.

Walter parked his small, rented car at the edge of the narrow, curvy road. Before shutting the door, he grabbed his knapsack and wide-brimmed hat. His hiking boots became dusty almost immediately as he walked toward a wall of exposed rock layers.

Approaching the wall, Walter was already glad for his hat that shielded him from the sun beating down on the mountainside. He set the knapsack on the ground and ran his fingers down the side of the wall. He drew a picture of what the layers looked like before taking any samples. The picture included some measurements, compass points, color descriptions, and the K-Pg Boundary, the line that separates layers of rock of the Cretaceous and Paleogene periods. As he finished the drawing, he took a drink of water and went on to his next task of collecting samples.

The chisel felt good in his hand and hitting the rock gently with the little hammer made a familiar clinking sound. As he chipped away, Walter would place each piece in a plastic bag and write on the bag where the rock had come from. He also added a note to his drawing describing where the rock sample came from. Later, he would send the samples to a lab where magnetic features would be analyzed.

As he continued his task of collecting samples, Walter kept getting distracted. Some fossils he noticed in the rock wall were

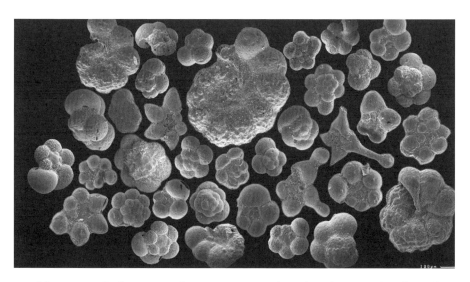

Highly magnified image of tiny Foraminifera fossil examples found in rock. Alvarez noticed that these fossils were different above and below the K-Pg boundary.

catching his attention. He sensed something unusual about the foram fossils he saw in the pink-colored rock.

Forams, or *foraminifera*, are tiny shells, remains of sea creatures found in beach sand and under the seas. Walter was looking at a wall of rock that had forams throughout every layer. The older ones, of course, were the ones on the bottom. Most people would be confused, seeing remains of sea creatures in the mountains, but that did not surprise Walter. He knew that this area had once been the bottom of a sea. Over millions of years, earthquakes had pushed the seafloor up to form the mountains where he was standing. What surprised Walter was the appearance of these forams.

In the lower layers of pink limestone, the forams were large

The iridium line that Walter Alvarez studied in Gubbio, Italy is everywhere on Earth. It is highly visible in Stevns Klint, Denmark. Compared to the pink rock in Gubbio, the K-Pg Boundary here appears light-colored. However, it is darker than the white cliffs in Denmark.

enough to be seen without a magnifying glass. But above the K-Pg Boundary, the forams were really tiny. This was curious.

The K-Pg Boundary contains a layer of light-colored, clay-like material, with no fossils in it. The material looked a bit like a chalk line drawn onto the cliffside. Walter had seen the K-Pg Boundary before, but now he found it to be more interesting than any other rock feature. He decided to focus his attention on that line.

Scientists all around the world were familiar with the K-Pg Boundary as the clay-like material can be found everywhere. Immediately below the line are the older Cretaceous rocks. These were formed during the time when dinosaurs roamed the Earth. Everyone knew that the dinosaurs had disappeared at the end of the Cretaceous Period, but in the 1970s, no one had any idea how or why they had died.

Immediately above the K-Pg line are rocks made during the Paleogene Period. Fossil hunters, professional and amateur alike, knew that dinosaur fossils could only be found below the line but never above it. There was something very strange about the K-Pg Boundary. Incredibly, no one before Walter had ever thought to investigate the line itself.

Walter thought that maybe whatever caused this weird clay-like line could be related to the change he saw in the size and shape of the forams. He reasoned that if he could tell how long it took that light-colored material to accumulate, he could tell how long it took the forams to change.

He knew that his father, Luis Alvarez, was just the man who could help him. Walter's father was a scientist too, a physicist who studied atoms. During World War II, Luis helped develop atomic weapons. He would have the equipment necessary to study the line in a way that had never been done before.

Carefully, Walter took samples of the clay-like rock from the K-Pg Boundary to his father to measure the rock's properties. Being able to work on a project that involved both sciences— Walter's geology and Luis' physics— was a rare occasion that the two men valued.

The father and son pair discussed many options to go about doing their task. Finally, they decided that measuring iridium in the sample would be the best way to tell how long it took for the clay line to form. Iridium is one of the rarest elements on Earth. It is more common to find it in rocks from outer space. Iridium accumulates in the soil at a known and constant rate. Once they knew the exact amount of iridium in the K-Pg Boundary material, they could calculate how long the change took.

What they found amazed them both. There was 30 times more iridium in the clay-like matter than in the rock layer above or below it. There was so much iridium in the sample that they shook their heads, unable to explain their findings. One thing they knew was that they needed to see if this extraordinary amount of iridium was only at the Gubbio site. *Was it possible that something strange had happened only in this area?*

Scientists sent them samples from faraway places like Denmark and New Zealand. Father and son were puzzled to find that even in these locations, there was an incredible amount of iridium in the K-Pg Boundary.

Realizing that the rare material was present in the dividing layer all over the world, Walter and his father started thinking the unthinkable. This could be the result of a global disaster! *Could it be that whatever caused the forams in the sea to change was related to the mass extinctions that had occurred at that time?*

The question the Alvarezes were asking now was, *What type of disaster could leave an iridium scar all over the planet?* They brainstormed possible answers. Luis knew what a large atomic explosion could do to the environment. This looked similar, but it was impossible. Atomic bombs had not been invented in prehistoric time. And even a nuclear bomb could not deposit a layer all over the globe!

Any worldwide catastrophe was difficult to imagine. No one had ever heard of such a thing before. Scientists base their ideas on observations. It just didn't seem "scientific" to think about global disasters.

Walter and his father couldn't escape the fact of iridium being a major feature of meteorites, which are rocks that fall to the ground from outer space. Thinking about whether a dust cloud caused by an impact could be carried through the air and coat the entire globe with iridium led them to their strange and startling conclusion: The dinosaurs were probably killed by a large asteroid impact. This would explain why dinosaur fossils were found only below the iridium-rich K-Pg Boundary line.

In June 1980, the Alvarezes published their findings in *Science Magazine*. The scientific community was stunned by this news. Most scientists did not accept the idea that the dinosaurs were killed by something from outer space. It sounded too strange, different from anything they had ever imagined. Even those who wanted to believe had a hard time accepting this idea. No one had ever found an impact crater large enough anywhere on Earth.

Finally, in 1991, after ten years of hunting for it, researchers located the crater where the asteroid hit. It had been very hard to find because it is located under the water off the coast of the Yucatan Peninsula, near the town of Chicxulub, in Mexico. At last, even the non-believers began to listen. Today, the vast

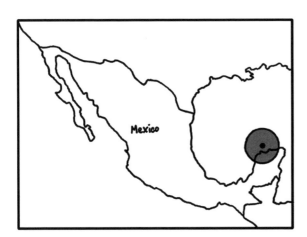

Site of the Chicxulub impact crater found off the coast of the Yucatan Peninsula, Mexico.

A piece of an asteroid blazing through the atmosphere. Asteroids tend to contain a large amounts of the rare element, iridium.

majority of scientists accept the Alvarezes' conclusion: The mass extinction at the end of the Cretaceous Period was caused by an asteroid hitting the planet.

The ability of Walter Alvarez and his father, Luis, to read the story in the rock didn't only change the way we look at the past, it changed the way scientists think about our Earth. We now know that gradual changes are sometimes punctuated by huge transformations. Thanks to Walter and Luis, school children around the world can learn the sensational story about an asteroid impact that caused the death of the dinosaurs.

Discussion

There are many jobs that involve exploring the secrets hidden under Earth's surface. Paleontologists figure out what animals from the past were like; archeologists study early humans, their architecture and how they settled around the globe; and geologists, like Walter Alverez, learn about Earth's past by uncovering evidence of earthquakes, volcanoes, glaciers, and the like. Which of these jobs would you prefer to do and why?

This image of Wegener smoking a pipe, was taken in Greenland in 1912.

CHAPTER 2

It Didn't Seem Possible

- Alfred Wegener

The *Glomar Challenger* was a drillship designed for deep sea research. This huge ship was equipped with a mechanism that could reach through five miles of salt water, all the way down to the bottom of the Atlantic Ocean. From the ocean's surface, the ship could drill out rocks that made up the ocean floor.

When the *Glomar Challenger* started its ocean research mission in 1968, most of the crew didn't know anything about Alfred Wegener, a man who had died 30 years earlier. But the geologists who knew of his far-fetched idea celebrated when the ship made its unusual findings. The rocks that the ship had attained from the bottom of the Atlantic Ocean uncovered the answer to the question Wegener posed so long ago.

Back in 1912, more than a half-century before the *Glomar Challenger* set out to sea, Alfred Wegener had an idea that was so outrageous that people couldn't believe it could possibly be true. He was an educated man who seemed to be interested in everything. In college, he studied physics (the study of motion), meteorology (the study of weather), and astronomy (the study of the stars). After he graduated, he continued to read a great deal about the latest scientific discoveries.

Wegener was studying the atmosphere in Greenland when he learned that fossils of tropical plants had been discovered in the icy country. This thought blew his mind. He knew how brutal the cold was up near the North Pole in Greenland and questioned how it was possible for tropical plants to grow there. *How could ferns*

This is what Greenland looks like. Yet, it is where fossils of tropical plants were found.

grow in a place where it is so cold that your breath condenses,
forming a little cloud in front of your face every time you exhale?
He thought that this recent finding might indicate that there was
once a global weather change, so he decided to investigate.

Wegener started reading more about fossils and looking
for possible evidence of climate change. His readings revealed
some interesting oddities such as scratches on rocks in areas
of Africa that appear to have been caused by glaciers! As he
smoked his pipe in his office, surrounded by piles of stacked
reading materials, he knew that these glacier scratches in tropical
Africa were just as weird as the fossils of tropical plants in icy
Greenland.

He looked at a map in one of his books, trying to figure out

how Greenland and Africa could have undergone such strange changes. Then he noticed what many children have noticed, probably since the first day that globes were put into classrooms. It seemed that if Brazil, a country in South America, could slide across the ocean over to the African shore, the two continents would fit together like puzzle pieces. Suddenly he had a thought: *Could Brazil and Africa actually have been joined? If they had been joined at one time, could this have something to do with the peculiarities recent reading had uncovered?*

The question drove him to read as much as he could about the area where Brazil and Africa seemed to connect. After reading many scientific papers, he came across an article about a reptile called the Mesosaurus. There were fossils of this little alligator-type creature, no more than 20 inches (50 cm) long, discovered in Brazil and in Africa, right where the two continents seem to fit together. Furthermore, these fossils were not found anywhere else in the world.

Puffing on his pipe, Wegener asked himself if it was possible that this reptile could swim across the Atlantic Ocean. However, he quickly put that idea aside because he reasoned that if a Mesosaurus could swim that far, fossils of them would have been found all over the place. In the end, Wegener thought that this was pretty good evidence that South America and Africa had once been joined together.

Artist's rendition of a Mesosaurus based on fossil evidence. Mesosaurus lived during the Early Permian Geologic Period. Fossils can be found in Africa and South America.

The Mesosaurus article inspired him to find out more about the rock at the fossil dig sites. He learned that the rock layers in Africa matched up with rock layers in South America. *How could that happen unless these rock layers were created together?*

Alfred Wegener was now convinced that the continents were once joined. And, if it were true that continents moved, there was no need to continue looking for signs of climate changes. Continents that moved from one climate to another would explain it all.

Armed with this evidence, he presented his idea to the scientific community, but no one could imagine that the continents moved. They asked Wegener how this was possible. Alfred Wegener had to admit that he didn't know. He could not explain how the continents moved; he just knew that they did.

The scientists thought there had to be other explanations for the tropical plant fossils in Greenland, glacial scratches in Africa, Mesosaurus fossils and matching rock layers found on opposite sides of the Atlantic Ocean.

Years went by and although many were intrigued by the evidence, they couldn't explain it. Then, one day, 30 years after Wegener's death, the *Glomar Challenger* revealed the explanation.

What scientists learned from the rock samples they collected was that the rocks in the middle of the ocean were some of the youngest rocks they had ever seen. Furthermore, they observed that if you started in the center

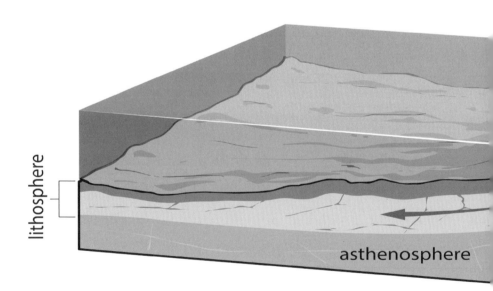

This image of plate tectonics under the ocean shows one plate moving away from the other.

of the Atlantic Ocean and moved toward the shore of South America or the shore of Africa, the rocks got older and older as you approached the continents.

The ship's findings provided the scientific community with the answer to Wegener's 50-year-old question about how the continents moved. New rock forming in the center of the ocean was pushing South America and Africa away from each other. Because the Atlantic Ocean is so wide, this pushing would have occurred over millions of years.

Sometime after Mesosaurus became extinct, when the fossils were already embedded in the rock, there were earthquakes that

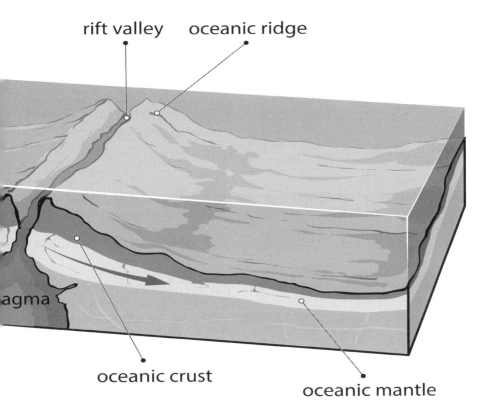

rift valley   oceanic ridge

magma

oceanic crust

oceanic mantle

created a huge crack, or rift, in the Earth. Some Mesosaurus fossils ended up on what would be the South American side of the rift and some ended up on the side that we would come to know as Africa. At the bottom of the rift, lava bubbled up. As it cooled, it hardened into new rock that held the two pieces of Earth away from each other. This process of earthquakes and lava turning to stone repeated. As the rift widened and deepened, it eventually filled up with water and became the Atlantic Ocean.

This rifting process didn't just make the Atlantic Ocean. It built mountains! The crack has bubbled up so much lava that it has built underwater mountains down the center of the Atlantic Ocean. The mountains are aptly called the Mid-Atlantic Ridge. To this day, activity at the Mid-Atlantic Ridge is causing the distance between South America and Africa to grow at a rate of about one inch (2 cm) per year. A similar process is happening at the Red Sea Rift, moving the Arabian Peninsula away from Africa.

As it turns out, all land masses on Earth are moving in a very slow process that we call plate tectonics. Finally, the mystery was solved. It took half a century to find out that Alfred Wegener's idea wasn't so far-fetched after all. It was just as he suspected – the continents move!

Discussion

If you were around at the time Wegener shared his evidence that the continents moved, would you have accepted that he was right, looked for other evidence (that might support or possibly disprove his claim), or would you simply reject his idea? Why would you have made that choice?

Mario Molina and his professor, Sherwood Rowland, reading a computer printout.

CHAPTER 3

Averting a Disaster

- Mario Molina

A boy named Mario Molina grew up and saved the world. You may not have been aware that our planet was ever in peril, but it was — until Mario Molina and a few of his friends discovered an enemy in the environment and came up with a plan to defeat it. They didn't use lasers or robots to fight the enemy. They used chemistry.

As a child in Mexico City in the 1950s, Mario loved science. He enjoyed viewing things under a microscope and playing with a chemistry set. He loved science so much that when he was old enough, he went to colleges in Mexico, Germany, and the United States to learn as much as he could about chemistry. He was awarded a doctorate in chemistry from the University of California Berkeley, and from then on, Mario was called Dr. Molina.

Armed with all the knowledge that modern science had to offer him, Dr. Molina was ready to fight off a chemical invader that he wasn't even aware of yet. When Molina was 30 years old, he was studying various molecules with Dr. Sherwood Rowland in a lab at the University of California's research facility in Irvine. Molina and Rowland were looking into how new chemicals impacted the environment, when an article about a group of molecules came to their attention: the molecules were called chlorofluorocarbons, or CFCs for short.

In the early 1970s, CFCs were used in cooling. They were in all the air conditioners in thousands of high-rise office buildings, all the refrigerators in homes, restaurants, and grocery stores. When used in spray cans, CFCs would allow the contents to spray out smoothly and evenly. They were in all the spray paint cans artists used for artistic expression and all the hairspray cans used to create the wild hairdos of the day. CFC molecules were literally everywhere!

At one time, many aerosol cans contained CFCs.

The CFC molecule is chemically inert, which means it doesn't interact with anything. It doesn't smell or catch fire. At first look, they seem to be perfectly safe. Molina and Rowland knew that as refrigerators and air conditioners age, they need to be recharged by adding CFCs. But they didn't know where the used CFCs that leaked into the environment ended up. Because CFC molecules are heavier than air, they thought that large quantities of the escaped molecules would be found near Earth's surface.

The article they read, however, said that CFCs were found in the stratosphere, over 12 miles above Earth's surface. It also said that because they were so far from the surface, they would be harmless. Molina and Rowland questioned this statement because they were aware of research being done by Dr. Paul Crutzen, a Dutch meteorologist. Crutzen had found another molecule, although not a CFC, in the stratosphere. He learned that conditions in the stratosphere caused the single molecule to split into two different molecules. His findings made Molina and Rowland wonder if this could be happening with CFCs in the stratosphere.

Molina and Rowland contacted Crutzen and the three of them started working together to see what was happening to CFCs. Crutzen helped verify that CFCs were in the stratosphere. The next step was to determine if they were truly harmless up there.

Because of his knowledge of chemistry, Molina was aware that many molecules change when exposed to the sun's rays,

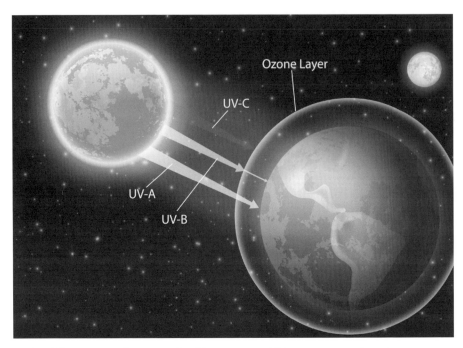

A healthy ozone layer will allow some UV-rays in – but it prevents harmful rays from entering.

like brightly-colored paper that fades after being exposed to sunlight. Molina also knew that the sun's rays are more intense in the stratosphere. So, he did some experiments. In the lab, Molina exposed CFCs to the same solar rays that they would experience in the stratosphere to see what would happen.

What he learned was that under the conditions in the stratosphere, the CFC molecule will come apart, releasing an unsafe chlorine atom. He was shocked to see these results, because chlorine is dangerous. It can break apart other molecules, including ozone molecules. The thought that chlorine could destroy ozone was very concerning to all three scientists because there is a layer of ozone molecules in the stratosphere that protects the entire Earth from the sun's harmful rays.

There are many rays that come from the sun. Among them are light, heat, and ultraviolet, also called UV. It is obvious that the sun hits us with visible light and with heat, but because we can't see it, UV is not so obvious. However, UV is just as important. UV light kills bacteria and your body uses it to produce Vitamin D. But too much of it causes sunburn and, in extreme cases, skin cancer. It's not the heat from the sun that will hurt your skin, it's the ultraviolet rays.

If you wear sunscreen with UV protection, you will still feel the warmth of the heat waves, but you will not get burned by the UV rays. A person on a tanning bed feels no heat, but if they stay in there too long, they will get a sunburn. Visible rays, heat rays, and ultraviolet rays come from the sun, but they all behave differently. The ozone layer protects the Earth by absorbing most of the hazardous UV light while allowing only a necessary amount to get through.

Without the ozone layer, life as we know it could not exist on this planet. That's how important it is. If the ozone were destroyed, we could protect ourselves from UV burns by wearing sunscreen or staying inside, but other living things would have no such protection. When plants suffer, so do every other living thing

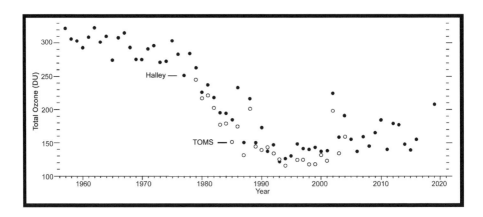

This graph shows data from instruments that measure ozone. Early measurements from ground instruments in Halley Bay, Antarctica show changing ozone levels. You can see a downward trend as early as 1976. Later, both the TOMS (Total Ozone Mapping Spectrometer) and the ground measurements from Halley Bay revealed continuous ozone depletion. In 1985, a hole in the ozone layer was announced. Current measurements suggest that the ozone layer is improving. (DU) means a column of ozone measured in Dobson Units. (Data courtesy of NASA)

— all food either comes from plants or things that have eaten plants. Thus, every life form depends on the ozone. Without it, the situation would be dire.

In 1974, Dr. Molina and Dr. Rowland wrote a paper and held a press conference to warn the public about the potential hazards of continuing to use CFCs. They explained that CFCs break apart and allow chlorine to destroy the ozone layer. But people didn't believe it. They needed proof. Two years later, ozone thinning was observed over Antarctica and the National Academies of Science reported that CFCs were destructive to the ozone layer. At that point, more people started paying attention, but many still believed that changes in the ozone could be a natural occurrence, and not due to the use of CFCs.

Molina did not give up. He continued to warn people, telling them that one atom of chlorine could go on destroying ozone, possibly for years, before degrading. He met with the U.S. Senate and with other government organizations. Finally, in 1985, the depletion of ozone could no longer be seen as a natural occurrence. Something had to be done. In 1987, which was 13 years after his initial plea, a ban on the production of CFCs was signed into law by 58 countries. Molina's persistence had finally paid off.

However, even after CFCs were banned, the hole in the ozone layer over Antarctica continued to grow just as Molina predicted it would. And, a second hole developed at the North Pole! What's worse is that people in Australia, which is close to the original hole, were reporting higher incidences of skin cancer. But eventually, thanks to the CFC ban, the damage slowed down and stopped. That doesn't mean things went back to normal; it just means that it stopped getting worse.

Imagine if Molina had not studied CFCs and the ozone in 1974. By the time 1987 came around, people would have just started looking into why the incidences of skin cancer were increasing. It might have been years before anyone considered looking at the ozone layer. Then, once they saw that the ozone was being destroyed, it would have taken even longer to realize that CFCs were causing the problem. And, throughout these years, CFCs would have continued to do damage. By then, it might have been too late, and the world would have been irreversibly damaged.

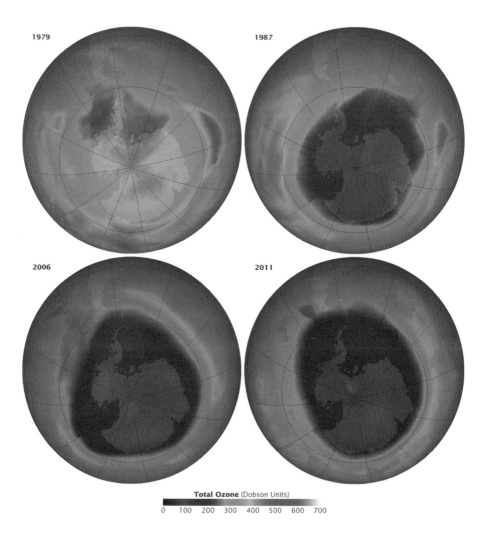

This image shows little or no thinning of the ozone layer in 1979, but as time went on, the hole above Antarctica grew larger, and then eventually stopped growing.

Instead, Dr. Molina got the ball rolling before the problem was out of control. Now that we've stopped accidentally adding chlorine into the stratosphere, the Earth seems to be healing itself. There is still a hole in the ozone layer above the South Pole, so it is advisable to wear sunscreen due to ozone thinning, but the situation is improving each day. Scientists believe that by the end of this century, the protective layer of ozone that surrounds the planet will be completely restored.

What almost happened to our planet is really scary. Mario Molina, together with his professor, Sherwood Rowland, asked an important question, looked for the answer, and didn't stop until they found it. They also continued to educate world leaders and the public until measures were taken to stop the production of CFCs, and a disaster was averted. In this way, one boy's love of science saved the world.

Discussion

Production of CFCs was banned once people realized that they were damaging the ozone. Today we face a similar problem: greenhouse gases that cause global warming. Do you think governments have the right to control the use of items such as gasoline that create greenhouse gases? Why or why not?

Tu Youyou, first Chinese female recipient of the Nobel Prize.

CHAPTER 4

An Ancient Chinese Remedy Gets New Life

- Tu Youyou

Tu Youyou grew up in China in the 1930s. As a teen, she was very sick with tuberculosis, a terrible, often deadly respiratory disease. There is a Chinese saying, "misfortune may actually be a blessing." Well, Tu's illness did turn out to be a blessing — for millions. It was her sickness that inspired her to study medicine, and although she didn't know it at the time, her name would one day be celebrated all over the world.

Tu was a chemist who specialized in learning how medicines were created. Since childhood, she had had an interest in age-old Chinese remedies and great respect for the traditional healers who came before. She knew that even though the ancients did not follow modern procedures to develop drugs, they would not have prescribed preparations that didn't have some curative properties.

Map showing the location of Vietnam.

Tu was almost 40 years old when the civil war between North and South Vietnam took place. The North was supported by China and other communist nations, while the United States and anti-communist countries backed the South. During that conflict, many soldiers from every army fell ill from a deadly disease called malaria.

Malaria is not caused by a bacterium or a virus. It is a sickness caused by a parasite, a living thing that takes advantage of another living thing to survive. Lice and leeches are parasites

What happens to a cell when the host catches malaria.

MALARIA

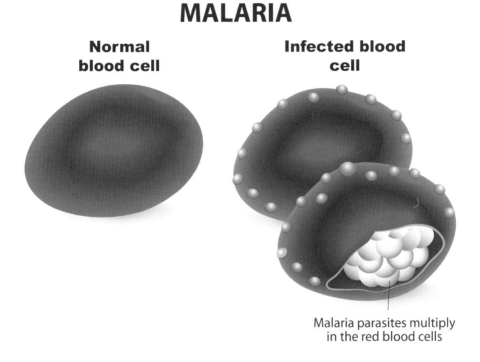

Normal blood cell

Infected blood cell

Malaria parasites multiply in the red blood cells

you might know about. Lice live in hair or feathers, where they chew and feed on skin. Leeches attach themselves to skin and suck their victims' blood. But as dreadful as these two parasites are, they are nothing compared to the malaria-causing parasite called plasmodium.

Plasmodium is microscopic and actually gets inside the body. It lives in, and gets nourishment from its victim's blood. Malaria is spread by the Anopheles mosquitos in tropical areas. When a mosquito carrying plasmodium bites a victim, the parasite is

This is a picture of the Anopheles species of mosquito that spreads malaria. No other species has been known to transmit the parasite.

transmitted into the victim's body where it feeds on his or her blood. What's worse is that once plasmodium is inside, it does what all living things do — it reproduces! A few weeks after being bitten, the victim develops a fever and becomes deathly ill. Malaria kills millions of people each year.

In 1968, there was already a treatment for malaria, a medicine called quinine. However, soldiers who took it were still dying at alarming rates. It was discovered that the malaria parasite, plasmodium, had become resistant to quinine. In response to this situation, the Chinese government immediately sent a call out to scientists all over China to work on solutions.

Early in 1969, Tu was dispatched to look for a new treatment. Because of her specialized interest, it became her role to investigate traditional Chinese remedies.

Tu began by finding as many ancient texts as she could. Wearing gloves so that the pages would not be damaged, she carefully opened each text, reading everything she could about the traditional remedies. She took notes and cross-referenced what she learned from various modern books. After a few months of researching this way, Tu had assembled a huge list of 640 materials with medical potential.

Once the list was compiled, it was decided that Tu would be responsible for screening the plants on the list while her team member would be responsible for screening mineral and animal sources. Tu's portion of the list included pepper plants and herbs such as sweet wormwood, a traditional Chinese medicine used to cure fever.

Tu gathered samples of various plants from her list. Then she extracted the active ingredients by boiling the plant samples in water. This procedure is similar

Artemisia annua plant native to Asia. It is sometimes called sweet wormwood and it often has tiny, round, prickly, yellow flowers (not shown).

to brewing tea. First, Tu snipped leaves from a plant, cut them into small pieces and allowed them to dry out. Then she boiled the dried leaves in water. Unlike brewing tea, however, accurate notes regarding the weight of leaves, water amounts, times, and temperatures needed to be recorded for hundreds of samples. These measurements were required because if any sample showed promise as a medicine, Tu and her group would need to be able to reproduce that exact extract. She labelled the samples and sent them to a government laboratory to be tested.

Two years and 120 tested samples later, the results did not match Tu's effort. After all that work, all she found was that pepper relieved malaria symptoms, but it could not stop the parasite. Nonetheless, it was time for Tu to participate in a large meeting where she and other scientists shared what they had been working on and what they learned.

After this meeting, Tu and many others were given new orders. She was no longer to send samples out to be tested. In addition to the job she was already doing, the testing of extract samples became her responsibility as well. To assist with this new task, three scientists were assigned to her. The group of four would explore the remaining herbs on Tu's list.

The responsibility of testing extract samples required her team to experiment on animals. There is simply no other way to determine whether a medicine works than to try it out on animals or people. Blood samples were taken from malaria-infected rats. The researchers would establish how much malaria was in the blood of each animal, inject an extract into the rat's blood, and at given times, see if the extract made any difference. The researchers realized the important role performed by the animals. Tu has said, "They have made great sacrifices for human health and deserve our reverence, compassion and gratitude."

As the team continued to test hundreds of extracts, Tu's focus narrowed to a plant called *Artemisia annua*, sometimes called sweet wormwood. Test results on *Artemisia annua* showed that it was no better than other plants. These results bothered Tu. She had had great hopes for this plant because nearly every traditional text she read had pointed to the use of *Artemisia annua*.

During the Ming Dynasty, *Artemisia annua* was listed as an anti-malarial treatment. There was also a story from 1,800 years ago about an army general who saved troops by instructing soldiers to keep a certain leaf in their mouths. From the description of the plant in the story, Tu suspected that it may have been *Artemisia annua*. However, her tests on *Artemisia annua* were not producing the results she had expected.

Tu did not give up. She read more texts and found a prescription written hundreds of years ago. It instructed the patient to soak many leaves in water for a while before drinking the water. This method took a long time and did not include heating. *This is curious*, she thought, *I wonder if there is another way?* Tu had to find a way to remove the extract that did not take as long. She also had to find a way to avoid heating which might damage the leaves.

This is when Tu had the first of two very creative ideas. She decided to boil the leaves in ether instead of water to remove the active ingredient. Ether is a clear, hazardous liquid with an awful smell. But its boiling point is barely above room temperature, far below the heat necessary to boil water. Using ether, she could boil the *Artemisia annua* leaves without overheating them, and boiling would be much faster than the soaking time required in the ancient prescription.

By changing the process to include ether, they now had to add another test into their already time-consuming procedure. They had to perform toxicity tests on animals to make sure that ether-treated *Artemisia annua* had no poisonous effects. Tu carefully injected the substance into healthy rats and was very pleased to learn that it did not harm any of them. Knowing that ether-treated *Artemisia annua* was not poisonous to rats, she could now use it to try to cure rats with malaria.

Unfortunately, team members were becoming ill from long-term exposure to ether, but they were willing to set aside their discomfort in order to find a cure. Then on October 4, 1971, Tu's

A modern-day research facility similar to where Tu worked.

group achieved overwhelming success: They had cured all the malaria-infected rats, with not a single side effect!

This was cause for celebration, but they still did not know if this treatment would be effective on humans. The team needed to test on other animals first, so they performed toxicity tests on healthy monkeys. When the monkeys showed no side-effects, they tested the extract on malaria-infected monkeys. Just like the rats, the monkeys were all cured. However, when they did the toxicity test on dogs, one of them had a bad reaction. It could have been an allergic reaction or it could have indicated that some animals find the potential medicine to be poisonous. Now what were they to do? It was not possible to continue tests using dogs because the extract may be dangerous to them. Some researchers suggested that they scrap the entire idea and return to testing pepper plants.

In spite of what happened with the dog, Tu was certain that *Artemisia annua*, extracted using ether, was safe. This is when she had her second brilliant idea — which was also a dangerous one. She volunteered to undergo the toxicity test herself! Her team, who had seen the incredible successes they had so far, quickly joined her. Their supervisors allowed them to volunteer, so in the summer of 1972, Tu and the three other scientists were injected with the extract. Luckily, no one had a bad reaction. They were all fine, which showed that ether-treated *Artemisia annua* was not toxic to humans. However, this still did not mean that it could cure human malaria victims. The final step was to treat malaria patients with the extract now called Artemisinin.

Twenty-one patients, in the Hainan Province of China, who were suffering from high fevers due to malaria were given Artemesinin. It was a success! Every one of them recovered! The hard work of Tu and her team had paid off. Almost immediately, large amounts of the miraculous Artemesinin were produced and sent to Africa where hundreds were suffering.

In 2015, Tu Youyou became the first Chinese female to win a Nobel Prize. When she accepted it, she shared the credit with all of the scientists on her team and all those involved in the project. Most would agree that as important as the Nobel Prize is, the real reward for Tu's efforts was Artemesinin itself. Thanks to the dedication of Chinese scientists, and Tu's brilliant, creative ideas, the anti-malaria drug Artemesinin has saved the lives of millions of people. It is now the standard treatment for malaria.

Discussion

What do you personally feel about Tu Youyou's decision to inject herself with untested medicine to see if it was poisonous? Was her action brave, confident, foolish, or something else? Explain your reasoning.

Henri Becquerel takes a rainy-day walk through Paris.

CHAPTER 5

Purely by Accident

- Henri Becquerel

When electric lights were a new invention, and the Wright Brothers were still fixing bicycles and attempting to fly, no one in the world knew that atoms or radiation existed. The year was 1895, and Wilhelm Röntgen had just discovered that there were invisible rays that could go through the human body to create an image of the bones inside. He called these mysterious rays "X-rays". Countless scientists were inspired to figure out this new X-ray phenomenon. Henri Becquerel was one of them.

Becquerel was a professor in the Department of Physics at the Paris National Museum of Natural History. After teaching his class, Becquerel would return to his book-filled office. Through the giant windows of the museum, Becquerel could see well-maintained gardens where colorful plants defined the edges of a long, wide walkway leading to the Seine River.

In this magnificent location, Becquerel had a large collection of phosphorescent materials that he had inherited from his grandfather, who had travelled around the world collecting them. Phosphorescence is a natural property of some minerals which allows them to absorb light and then emit light in darkness. Modern glow-in-the-dark paint contains phosphorescent minerals. When the light is on, the minerals absorb the light so that when the light is turned off, the phosphorescent paint glows.

Becquerel knew that his glow-in-the-dark minerals gave off light and he knew that X-rays left a picture on film the way light did. He wondered if there was a connection between X-rays and phosphorescence. The idea excited him. He couldn't wait to set up an experiment to explore the possibility. His experiment would test whether his glow-in-the-dark samples could also expose film the way X-rays had.

Before digital cameras, film was used to capture an image. In Becquerel's time, film was a glass plate covered by a layer of light-sensitive silver crystals. When the crystals were exposed to light, or invisible X-rays, the film would turn dark. If Becquerel prevented light from getting to the film by wrapping the plate in dark cloth, the silver crystals would not be activated – nothing would happen. But X-rays were known to go right through the dark cloth and darken the film.

To see whether his minerals would expose the film, Becquerel carefully put one jar of phosphorescent material onto a wrapped film plate. He then put both together in the sunlight that shined onto his desk next to the window. In the sun, the glow-in-the-dark mineral could absorb sunlight. If his samples were related to X-rays, the glow from the sample inside the jar would penetrate the covered plate and leave a darkened spot where the jar had been.

Jars of glow-in-the-dark materials similar to those in Henri Becquerel's collection. They absorb light and then glow in darkness. Most of these types of materials are not radioactive; Henri just happened to have one that was.

He tested dozens of jars of phosphorescent minerals and salts in this way. But he was disappointed when they did not expose the film. There were no dark spots on the plates in any of his first tests.

However, when he tried a glow-in-the-dark uranium salt, he got a different result. The film under that sample was exposed. He didn't understand why the other samples did not expose the film, but this one did. It puzzled him. He thought he must have

This is the actual image Becquerel created by placing a coin between his jar of uranium salt and the wrapped photographic plate. (Photograph courtesy of Henri Becquerel, 1903, in: Recherche sur une propriété nouvelle de la matière.)

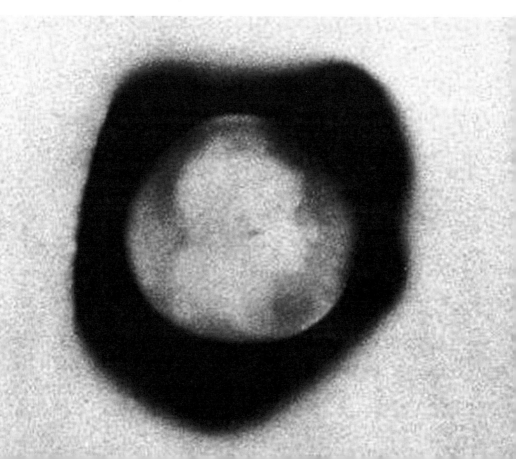

done something wrong, so he repeated some of the earlier-tested samples. He hoped that they would expose the film the way the uranium salt had. But again, he saw nothing. He began to think that maybe his idea that glow-in-the dark materials were related to X-rays was incorrect. He also wondered if the positive results he got with uranium salt were caused by a mistake he made while testing that sample. He knew he would need to re-test the uranium salt.

On the day Henri Becquerel was to repeat the uranium salt experiment, he became concerned about the possible outcomes. It worried him that if the uranium showed nothing, he would have to admit to himself that the idea that excited him so much was wrong. And, if the uranium salt exposed the film as it had the first time, he would be in the same position he was in right now. He had no explanation for what he saw. He really needed to think about something else for a while.

As luck would have it, just as he started setting up the experiment to re-test the uranium salt, the sky darkened, threatening to rain. Without sunlight, his uranium test would have to wait for another day. He placed the covered photographic plate along with the jar of uranium salt into the drawer of his oversized, wooden desk. Then he grabbed his coat and umbrella, and went for a walk.

Paris was beautiful on that chilly, overcast, February day. Ancient stone bridges spanned the shores of the Seine. The light from lanterns caused the raindrop speckled water below to shimmer.

As Becquerel strolled, horse-drawn carriages navigated both sides of the shiny, wet streets. Men in knee-length overcoats and stovepipe hats, along with women wearing long dresses and shawl-topped coats, carried black umbrellas across the promenades. The recently-built Eiffel Tower, to the west, was not visible through the rainy-day clouds. Across the river, people escaped the rain by visiting the Louvre Museum, the former royal palace, to see DaVinci's famous painting, the *Mona Lisa*. There were many things to do, even on rainy days, in the City of Lights.

Paris continued to be sunless, raining on and off for an entire week. The time allowed Becquerel to clear his head and be ready for whatever results the uranium test produced. When the sunshine returned, Becquerel opened the drawer containing the plates and the jar of uranium salt. He decided to process this film.

What he saw shocked and perplexed him. The film that had been in the darkness of the drawer had somehow became exposed! He couldn't believe it. After wondering in disbelief for a while, he tucked the uranium salt sample back into the drawer with a new plate to see what would happen. When he checked five hours later, he was puzzled to find the new plate was exposed too. The uranium salt was not in any light, so it was not glowing. Even so, it darkened the film.

He performed this experiment a few more times just to make sure that what he saw really happened. Then, once he was sure he hadn't made a mistake, he began doing experiments to learn as much as he could about this mystery. It seemed like the uranium might be emitting some kind of rays. He put things between the jar of uranium and the film-plate to see what would happen. The mysterious, invisible rays penetrated paper and exposed the film. The rays were captured by the film as if the paper had not been there. When he put a coin between the uranium and the plate, it left a faint shadow of the coin, complete with a face, on the film. When he put a cross-shaped, metal medallion between the film-plate and the jar of uranium, the result was extraordinary. The film showed a darkened circle caused by the uranium and there was a light cross-shape from the medallion in the center of the darkened area. The metallic medallion had stopped the rays from getting through. Henri Becquerel took very accurate notes on all of his experiments and presented the notes along with the images to the scientific community. His colleagues were intrigued. Many returned to their own labs to reproduce his results.

Becquerel's rays, as they were referred to for some time, eventually came to be called radioactivity. This radioactivity is naturally released by uranium. It was just a coincidence that uranium salts also phosphoresce. That's why uranium salt was included with his other glow-in-the dark materials. Most

Becquerel, who shared the 1903 Nobel Prize with Pierre and Marie Curie, was commemorated with the Curies on this Swedish postage stamp in 1963.

phosphorescent materials are not radioactive. We have come to learn that uranium and three dozen other elements, including radium, thorium, and polonium, are all radioactive and will darken film. Most of these elements were not discovered until after Becquerel's experiments.

Becquerel's rays were not X-rays. It turns out that what Becquerel saw were the tiny energetic particles released by radioactive elements. Becquerel was not aware of the dangers of handling uranium and he suffered some ill-effects, like mysterious burns on this hands, from working with it.

Today we harness radioactive energy to help diagnose and treat diseases, power submarines, determine the age of rocks, and kill bacteria. Radioactivity is a clean, non-carbon-emitting, form of electricity used in many cities. Becquerel's Paris, the City of Lights, powers those lights almost exclusively with radioactive energy. In fact, about 75% of all of the electricity used throughout France today comes from radioactivity.

Henri Becquerel discovered this amazing form of energy purely by accident. He might not have ever seen it at all, if rain hadn't forced him to take a break.

Discussion

Becquerel discovered radioactivity. Good things about radioactivity include its ability to provide clean electricity to power cities and radioactivity also makes X-rays and other medical diagnostic and treatment tools possible. However, without his discovery, such things as atomic bombs and power plant accidents capable of serious destruction would not exist. Overall, do you still believe that radioactivity is good for humanity?

Florence Nightingale, "The Lady with the Lamp", during the Crimean War.

CHAPTER 6

How One Nurse Saved Millions of Lives

- Florence Nightingale

In 1854, photographs from the Crimean War, sometimes referred to as The War of the Empires, were printed in the British newspapers. In this massive conflict, horses pulled cannons and soldiers used swords or smokey rifles. The Russian, English, French, and Ottoman (Turkish) Empires were fighting over religious beliefs and for control of the land along the Black Sea. For the first time in history, families who had loved ones fighting in a faraway conflict could see the horrors that their sons and brothers were facing. People all over the world felt powerless reading about the war, but there was a young woman, a nurse named Florence Nightingale, who believed it was her destiny to help.

This image is of the type of smokey cannon used in the Crimean War.

Nightingale had known that she had wanted to be a nurse since she was 17 years old. Her parents, however, did not like this idea and tried to talk her out of it. Her family was quite wealthy, so Nightingale grew up surrounded by luxury. She was provided with an education that included the languages, mathematics, and philosophy. Her parents saw nursing as work unfitting for a lady and they wanted to shield her from those unpleasantries. They expected her to marry a wealthy man.

However, Nightingale chose a completely different path than what her parents envisioned. She rejected a marriage proposal and instead set her sights on nursing. There were no nursing schools at that time, so Nightingale educated herself by working with doctors at a Lutheran Hospital in Germany, before going on to learn more in Paris, after which she returned to London to begin her career.

Nightingale explained to her parents that she believed God had called her to do the necessary work of healing the sick. Hearing this, her parents still didn't like the idea, but came to respect her decision.

Working as a nurse at Middlesex Hospital in London, Nightingale's dedication to patient care and her managerial abilities quickly earned her a promotion and a reputation. Like everyone else in the city, she followed the news of the Crimean War closely. The photographs were shocking. The dreadful images and the accounts of disease and death made her wonder how her nursing talents could be used to help the young men suffering in the war.

The answer came to her in the form of a letter from the Secretary of War. In the letter he explained that he had heard of her ability to get things done and he asked if Nightingale could organize a corps of nurses to treat hospitalized soldiers in the war zone.

Nightingale was quick to respond. She talked to leaders at her church about going to the front to help the soldiers, and she asked her fellow nurses. Soon, she had amassed 38 volunteer women who wanted to bring their knowledge, compassion, and help to the distant front.

The trouble was that no female in European history had ever treated wounded soldiers in a war zone. Military personnel and even the doctors, who were all male, would be uncomfortable having women there. Nightingale and her group were only allowed to go to Turkey because they had correspondence from the Secretary of War.

Nightingale's desire to go to a battlefield to help soldiers was beyond her parents' worst fears. They were devastated. They never imagined that their daughter would be working in a war zone.

The world didn't know it yet, but Nightingale was exactly the right person to lead the group of volunteers. She was perfect because London had recently undergone a cholera epidemic and Nightingale had first-hand experience treating the victims at the hospital where she worked.

At that time, no one knew about germs being the cause of disease, but Nightingale and others learnt that clean water and clean conditions were the key to avoiding illness. Sickness is often referred to as the second enemy, as bacteria thrive in the filthy conditions created by war. One incredibly sad statistic shows that in the Crimean War, British soldiers were four times more likely to die from disease than from battle wounds!

When the women arrived at the huge hospital in Turkey toward the end of 1854, they were greeted by an unbearable stench. The building was three stories tall and had a central courtyard that was used as a garbage dump. Inside, the smell of disease made it worse, and the deafening sounds of artillery fire became background noise to the moans of the wounded soldiers. Sick beds in the overcrowded hospital were crammed so close together that there was barely room to walk around to serve these unfortunate victims.

Due to cholera, some men were vomiting, and others had diarrhea, but they were too sick or seriously wounded to get out of bed. The nurses worked furiously to keep up, constantly emptying pails, mopping floors, and laundering and changing bed sheets.

Getting clean water was also an issue. Nightingale sought additional help from some Turkish women, but the need was still overwhelming. On a few occasions, she wrote to *The Times*, a London newspaper, letting them know what was happening and what was needed. Citizens of Britain responded generously to her requests for bandages and supplies.

The nurses and other women tackled monumental tasks. In addition to nurses busily assisting in bloody surgeries and directly treating the sick, all of the women moved garbage, washed walls, and fixed leaks. The people in the hospital quickly came to appreciate all the women at the Turkish front for their work and skill.

In spite of her fatigue as evening approached, Nightingale would take a moment every day to write down what she had seen. She didn't do this in any usual way. Too exhausted to keep a diary and too emotionally drained to record each man's name, she used her mathematics skills. She created a polar area diagram, a large circular graph, and filled it in each night. The graph was divided into 12 sections, like a clock, one section for each month. At the beginning of the month, she would start in the center and build outward, indicating how many soldiers died from injuries and how many died from disease each day.

Florence's faith that she was doing God's work kept her focused and strong for an entire year despite the conditions. Once she had records for an entire year, she noticed that the summer months had fewer deaths from disease. She did not know why the summer months were better, but she thought it might be because the windows were open in the summertime. In response to this idea, she made changes. She introduced more fresh air and sunlight into the hospital in the winter by opening the windows wide, in spite of the cold temperatures outside and all the protests from those inside. Each night she continued to graph her data.

When she finished her nightly tally, after many of the staff had gone to bed, she would make her evening rounds administering to patients while carrying a Turkish lantern before going to bed. This practice earned her the nickname "Lady with the Lamp."

Nightingale and her crew saved the lives of hundreds, perhaps thousands, during the war. The number of soldiers who died declined significantly once the women began their nursing mission at the front. However, Nightingale saved even more lives after the war. She did this in two ways.

First, she opened the world's first nursing school, St. Thomas' School for Nurses in London, which was later renamed The Nightingale Training School in her honor. There, she educated nurses about the benefits of cleanliness and fresh air for patients. Through her much-publicized efforts during the war, Nightingale

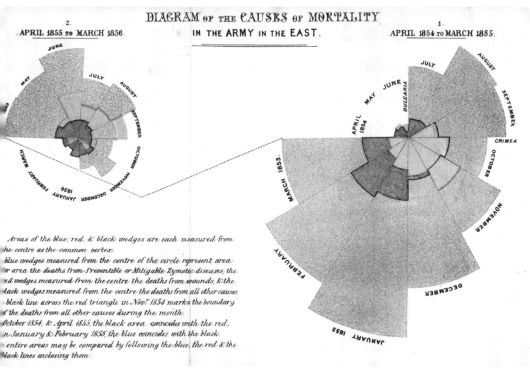

DIAGRAM OF THE CAUSES OF MORTALITY IN THE ARMY IN THE EAST.

These are the graphs Florence Nightingale presented to Parliament. Light gray areas represent deaths by disease. Even though the graphs are different sizes, you can see that there is more light gray on the earlier (right side) graph during the winter (bottom) months. (Courtesy of H. Martineau and F. Nightingale, 1859, in England and her Soldiers.)

had made nursing a respected profession. This attracted many young women to go into nursing, some wealthy like herself. Her students went on to work and teach around the globe, undoubtedly saving countless lives.

Secondly, Nightingale continued saving lives after the war with her statistical data. She presented her graphs, now called Nightingale's Rose Diagrams because their shape resembles a rose, to the British Parliament. Her visual representation of the number of deaths caused by disease and graph showing fewer deaths in the months of summer as compared to winter after she opened the windows and cleaned up the garbage, were easy to understand. They convinced Parliament that things needed to change. Laws were put into place requiring property owners to improve sanitation and clean up messes. Public health improved almost immediately all over England. The improvements were so remarkable that other countries adopted the same changes suggested by Nightingale's data. Significant changes were made in India, and, just a few years later, during the U.S. Civil War, Nightingale was consulted regarding the state of army hospitals.

The Lady with the Lamp is often credited with being an incredible nurse, but people sometimes forget her other contributions. She single-handedly started the profession of modern nursing. She was a scientist and statistician, who collected data and drew conclusions from it to focus on the cause of disease. She was a powerful activist who changed public policy beyond the borders of her own country. Even as she aged and grew ill, she continued teaching and advocating for public health. Florence Nightingale was a rich woman who surrendered a life of wealth and leisure to dedicate her efforts to caring for others. Her nursing techniques continue to save millions of lives. What she gave the world was priceless. It is worth more than all her wealth could have achieved.

Discussion

Florence Nightingale prevented soldiers from dying. Do you think helping soldiers live through wars will make war in the future more or less likely?

Photograph of Alexis St. Martin at approximately 70 years of age. (Photograph Courtesy of Jesse Shire Meyer, 1912, in Life and Letters of Dr. William Beaumont.)

CHAPTER 7

They Struck a Deal

- Alexis St. Martin & Dr. Beaumont

About two hundred years ago, on a tiny island nestled in Lake Huron, a terrible accident occurred that would affect medical history. This place is called Mackinac Island and it lies in U.S. waters near the Canadian border, where the Great Lakes become icy cold in the winter.

If you visit the island today, it takes little effort to envision the days gone by. There are no cars on the entire island. To this day, residents use horses and buggies to get around. There are also many places on Mackinac that have been left completely natural and untouched. In the fall, noisy Canada geese stop there to rest on their journey. The water reflects the gorgeous colors of the leaves from the forest above. In this setting, it's easy to imagine a canoe floating by.

The original army fort on Mackinac Island still stands high on a hill with its black iron cannons pointed out towards the water.

By looking at the structure, which is now a museum, one would know that it was once a powerful fortification used to protect the island and its strategic location between two countries. School children learn that Fort Mackinac was the site of the first military encounter in the War of 1812.

After that bloody battle, there was a time of peace before the American Civil War. During this quiet time, before the California gold rush, when the United States had only 24 states, fur trappers would come to the island by canoe. They came north from woodlands in America and south from Canadian forests to sell their wares in a growing, little town on Mackinac Island.

This map shows the location of Mackinac Island, a Michigan island, in Lake Huron.

Artist's rendition of what Mackinac Island looked like on the day Alexis St. Martin arrived.

There, Native Americans, Frenchmen and U.S. soldiers lived and worked together.

On a beautiful spring day during that peaceful time in 1822, a French-Canadian fur trapper named Alexis St. Martín was on the island to sell his fur pelts. Working alone, it was the young man's job to set animal traps and come back some time later to retrieve the dead animals. He would then skin them – cooking and eating some while leaving the others for forest animals – pack the skins into his canoe, and venture south across the lonely expanse of cold Lake Huron to trade the furs he collected.

At the foot of the Fort Mackinac hill, across from a huge vegetable garden that produced enough food for the army

As a young man, St. Martin trapped animals and then travelled alone across Lake Huron to sell the animal pelts on Mackinac Island.

residents, stood The American Fur Company. The building was about thirty feet wide and twenty feet deep. On each end was a chimney for the two very necessary fireplaces within. The interior had only two rooms. The small room on the left was used to store traded furs that would ultimately be shipped to Europe and elsewhere. The larger room was retail space.

Alexis entered this trading post with his pelts. Directly in front of him was a large wooden counter with a cash register. Every available wall space in this retail area was filled with shelves containing supplies such as pots, blankets, tobacco and a variety of other things that he could trade for his pelts. On that day, the shop was busy, filled with other traders.

While Alexis stood in the shop preparing to trade, another patron set a shotgun on the counter. Suddenly, "Kablam!" The sound of the gun thundered in the small room and Alexis was thrown to the floor. The gun had accidentally fired, hitting him in the belly from only a few feet away! Immediately, shouts erupted and the townspeople ran up the long incline to the fort above, to get the army doctor. The doctor grabbed his coat and medical bag and was instantly outside following the messengers down to help the victim. All of them scurried quickly but cautiously as the incline could cause them to fall.

Dr. Beaumont arrived in the store to find Alexis lying on the floor bleeding from a hole in his torso. The wound was roundish, about 4 inches (or 10 centimetres) across. Through the hole, the doctor could see a broken rib and a damaged lung. He skillfully amputated the broken rib and tucked the lung back into place. Then he carefully removed all of the shotgun pellets, stopped the bleeding, and dressed the wound.

A cot was set up for Alexis in the American Fur Company building. It would have been far too dangerous to try to move him all the way up the hill to the fort in his condition. Every day, the doctor took the sloping trip down to the fur company to tend to his patient. Dr. Beaumont changed bandages and kept Alexis comfortable before climbing back to the fort.

The problem was that whenever the young man tried to eat, much of the contents of his stomach would ooze out of the wound onto the bandages. When Alexis developed a fever, medicines were useless because, like food, most would spill out onto the bandages. The doctor did not tell anyone his thoughts at the time, but later he would reveal that he did not expect the young man to survive.

Nonetheless, Dr. Beaumont visited his patient every day and he quickly learned how to compress the wound so that food could remain in. Once the fever was gone and food could be held inside, Dr. Beaumont offered to sew the wound closed but Alexis, having already suffered so much pain and trauma, would not allow it.

One year after the accident, to everyone's surprise, Alexis was alive and well. Actually, it depends on how you define well. His wound, which was now much smaller, about 2.5 inches (6 centimetres), had healed in an unusual way. Instead of one side fusing to the other, the edges all around the wound had healed, leaving a visible opening to the young man's stomach! The doctor continued to compress and bandage the wound so that the contents of Alexis' stomach would stay inside.

Then in the winter of 1823-24, almost a year and a half since the blast, Alexis' wound continued to heal in a most extraordinary and unexpected way. A small fold, or doubling, of the stomach lining appeared inside toward the top of Alexis' stomach. The fold continued to drop downward until it completely covered the hole!

Thanks to this natural healing, Dr. Beaumont no longer had to apply bandages in order for food to stay in. On the surface, Alexis' wound appeared to be a round indentation in his skin, nothing more. But the stomach lining covering the wound now acted as a flap. By pushing in on the flap, the inside of the stomach could still be seen. Once this healing occurred and food could stay in, Alexis was determined to be in good physical condition. However, it was not advisable for the young man to return to working alone in the woods, so Alexis and Dr. Beaumont struck a deal.

Alexis agreed to work as a handyman for the doctor who would provide medical care, if needed. In return, Alexis would allow the curious doctor to do experiments with his stomach! Alexis also agreed to travel to universities and hospitals with Dr. Beaumont to show other doctors the unusual injury. In 1823, little was known about the process of digestion.

As a handyman, Alexis chopped wood and carried packages. He also did yardwork and whatever small chores the doctor needed. Dr. Beaumont, as planned, performed experiments using Alexis' exposed stomach. Incredibly, Dr. Beaumont was able to observe the churning motions of the young man's internal stomach walls. He could see a living stomach as it worked!

The doctor would tie a piece of string around a measured, weighted piece of food and place it in Alexis' stomach. Then at a given time later, Dr. Beaumont would pull the string and examine what had happened to the food particle on it. From these experiments, the doctor learned that digestion was caused by acids in the stomach. He also learned that the acid was secreted by the stomach lining.

For one experiment, Dr. Beaumont touched the inside of the exposed stomach with his tongue several times over the course of a few days. The taste revealed that an empty stomach does not have acid; food entering the stomach is what triggers acid production.

By carefully inserting a thermometer into Alexis's stomach, Dr. Beaumont also learned that the inside of the stomach is a bit warmer, about 1°F higher, than normal body temperature. Dr. Beaumont also did experiments with the stomach acid itself. He would remove a bit of acid and put it in a jar with food or other materials. He learned that digestion happened at different speeds depending on whether Alexis had eaten vegetables or meats, and whether he had been exercising or resting.

For almost ten years, Alexis worked as the doctor's handyman. As they travelled the country together, the doctor continued to do experiments. But when Dr. Beaumont was to relocate to St. Louis, Alexis decided that it was time to go back home to Canada.

William Beaumont published his meticulous research in a book entitled, *Experiments and Observations on the Gastric Juice and the Physiology of Digestion.* The book changed the way doctors understood digestion and earned Dr. Beaumont the nickname "Father of Gastric Physiology." Furthermore, it changed the way the medical community did research. Until this incident, doctors did research by observing what was happening on the outside of the patient. This was the first time that the inside of a living body could be observed.

Alexis St. Martin, after returning home to Canada, married and had a family. He lived to be an old man and died of natural causes 58 years after his near-fatal shotgun wound. His contribution to medical science was great. He did something truly wonderful for humanity by allowing his unfortunate circumstances to be explored in the interest of increasing human knowledge.

Discussion

Do you think it was ethical for Dr. Beaumont to experiment on Alexis St. Martin? Do you think experiments on humans should be allowed today? If so, to what extent and with what restrictions?

Dr. Daniel Hale Williams, founder of Provident Hospital in Chicago.

CHAPTER 8

The Barber's Son

- Daniel Hale Williams

Daniel Hale Williams was an African-American boy who was born in the free state of Pennsylvania in 1856, just before the American Civil War. As a child, Williams aspired to grow up to be a barber like his dad, but a barber shop customer would encourage him to take a different path. History would show that the path taken by Daniel Hale Williams was exceptional.

Growing up in the small town of Hollidaysburg, Williams often sat in the barber shop while his father worked. He listened to men who worked in mines, foundries, and on the docks as they discussed what was in the news. Newspapers told of Abraham Lincoln becoming President, and they reported on the Battle of Fort Sumter which set off the Civil War. The men shared news about dozens of battles that followed. When Williams was seven years old, the bloodiest battle of the Civil War was fought in Gettysburg, only 120 miles southeast of where he lived.

By 1866, the war was finally over. This should have been a good year, but for Williams, it was the year his father died from tuberculosis. This loss shattered his family. His mother, unable to care for all seven of her children, placed some of them with relatives. Williams was sent to Baltimore, where he learned to shine shoes. He hated his job, and wondered whether he would ever get to be a barber.

Fortunately, within a few years, Williams was able to rejoin his family and spend the rest of his childhood in Rockford, Illinois. Then, at age 20, he moved away on his own to Janesville, Wisconsin, where he finally got the chance to work as a barber. The smell of hair tonics, the ringing of the bell above the door, and the sound of men crinkling newspapers and talking about the day's events made him feel right at home.

It was in this barber shop that Williams befriended a customer, Dr. Henry Palmer, a local physician who had served in the Civil War. The doctor saw a hidden talent in Williams.

The Civil War had resulted in black people being freed from slavery, but segregation occurred every day. There were "whites only" water fountains, seats on buses were segregated, and black people were not allowed in many restaurants. What was worse is that, in the 1800s, African-American patients were not allowed in the "white only" hospitals, and although a great need existed for black doctors, colleges would not train them. The situation was dire.

From the conversations in the barber shop, Dr. Palmer knew that Williams had done quite well in school, especially in mathematics and the sciences. He also noticed that Williams was a careful listener as customers described their needs. Shaving a man's curved face with a straight blade is difficult, and even experienced barbers would sometimes accidentally scrape or nick a client's face. However, Williams' eyes were so keen and his hands so steady that he never nicked anyone. It was this natural gift that caught Dr. Palmer's attention.

Dr. Palmer believed Williams had the qualities necessary to be an excellent surgeon. The idea was a radical one to Williams. But after talking with the experienced physician, Williams considered the possibility. He enjoyed being a barber, and looked forward to it for some time, but maybe it was possible to do something greater. Saving lives would be far more important than making sure a man was well-groomed. Williams knew that his father would have been proud of this decision.

So, he worked as an apprentice to Dr. Palmer who helped him get into Chicago Medical College. There, Williams attended classes, studied hard, and successfully graduated as a doctor in 1883. Medical specialties did not exist at that time. Any physician who assisted in an operation and felt confident enough to do so could then perform surgeries on their own.

The newly-certified Dr. Williams, like all doctors back then, made house calls, and it was sometimes necessary to perform surgeries in a patient's kitchen. This practice was especially common in black communities because no hospitals would admit African-Americans at the time. In these conditions, Dr. Williams gained a reputation as being a fine physician. He delivered babies, quieted fevers, set broken bones, wrapped burns, and stitched-up cuts. He was very good at preventing infections in his patients.

As his reputation grew, he explained to the medical community how important it was to provide education for African-American doctors and nurses. He was one of the only black doctors practicing in Chicago, a city of over half a million people with a black population that was growing steadily since the end of the Civil War.

When a young, black woman told Dr. Williams that she had been denied entrance into nursing school because of the color of her skin, Williams knew that a new kind of hospital and training facility was needed. He gathered black ministers and physicians and discussed the possibility of opening their own hospital.

Williams was an active member of the Illinois State Board of Health and he was a good speaker. Appealing to the membership, he was able to secure some funds for his hospital. Armour Meat Packing Company, one of Chicago's most important businesses and an employer of many emancipated slaves, provided the down payment for a three-story brick structure. With these contributions and generous support from the community, Dr. Williams opened Provident Hospital. The Chicago hospital was the first multi-racial health facility in the United States. There, doctors and nurses of every ethnicity were trained, and no patients, regardless of race, were turned away.

One night in 1893, after Dr. Williams had been working as a general surgeon in Provident Hospital for a few years, a patient named James Cornish was rushed in, bleeding severely. Cornish had been in a bar fight and suffered a very serious stab wound. There was a deep cut right into his chest. Dr. Williams knew that this man would die without immediate help.

Similar injuries had been seen by other doctors, but it was commonly believed that all that could be done in this situation was to make the patient comfortable in their last moments. Stab wounds to arms or legs

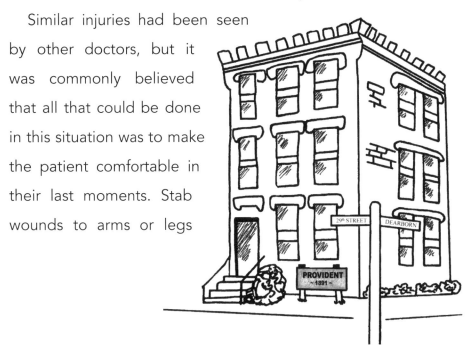

Artist's rendition of the original Provident Hospital (1891) on 29th Street and Dearborn in Chicago.

could be stitched-up, but a chest wound was different. There were ribs, multiple tissue layers, and there was a great deal of blood obscuring what a doctor could see. With only ether as anesthesia and no antibiotics, heart surgery certainly appeared to be impossible.

However, Dr. Williams was not willing to give up on his patient. Williams did not have the advantage of any modern surgical equipment, or a medical textbook to advise him on how to proceed, but the skilled doctor addressed each challenge as he encountered it.

After administering ether to anaesthetize Cornish, Dr. Williams sliced into Cornish's skin and pulled back the ribs. By continuously dabbing up the blood, Dr. Williams could see that Cornish's artery had been cut in the attack. Arteries carry blood from the heart to the rest of the body. As long as this bleeding continued, the rest of the body would be denied life-giving, oxygen-rich blood. There was no time to waste.

Dr. Williams carefully stopped the bleeding by quickly sewing the artery closed. He followed the same procedure that he would for an injured artery anywhere else in the body, but there was still a great deal of bleeding.

By continuously dabbing up blood, he was able to see that there was an inch-long gash in his patient's pericardium. The pericardium is a thick, protective layer of tissue surrounding the

Drawing of the human heart. Lighter arrow shows the path of oxygen-depleted blood that gets pumped to the lungs to be replenished. Darker arrow shows the path of oxygen-rich blood that comes from the lungs and gets pumped into arteries that distribute it throughout the body.

Labels on diagram: Arteries to Body; Veins to Heart; To Lungs; From Lungs

entire four-chambered heart.

Countless times in the past, Dr. Williams had listened with his stethoscope as blood passed through the four chambers of patients' hearts. But today, for the first time, he was actually looking at a living heart rhythmically expanding and contracting as it worked!

Seeing the damage on this rapidly pulsating heart, Williams was not surprised that his patient was also having trouble breathing. Used blood enters the heart and gets pumped to the lungs where waste is replaced with oxygen. The bleeding gash in the heart was causing the entire heart-lung system to fail. The entire body would soon fail and the patient would die if the gash wasn't closed immediately.

Without delay, Dr. Williams sewed the cut in that outermost layer while the heart was still beating! Then he closed it securely with tough fishing line. Dr. Daniel Hale Williams had just performed the very first documented heart surgery in the United States!

Approximately seven weeks after the surgery, James Cornish returned home healthy. He did not die that day but instead lived 20 more years, thanks to Dr. Williams' dedication and willingness to save his life.

Dr. Daniel Hale Williams is an inspiration. He grew up in a bleak town during a war and lost his father at an early age. To benefit humanity, he had to tackle segregation and prejudice. Yet, he overcame these obstacles and opened the first African-American owned and operated hospital in the United States. Here, persons of all races were trained to be doctors and nurses. In this three-story building with twelve patient beds, Dr. Williams also performed a ground-breaking heart surgery.

His hospital is still in operation. It is in a new facility in Chicago, near where the old building stood, and today it is known as Provident Hospital of Cook County. It currently employs 450 full-time persons, and heart surgeries are routine. It is a large building and there are plans for a new, modern, eight-story structure that will include more outpatient services, labs, and a new emergency department with 18 bays. The hospital continues to serve and train persons of all races and provides charity care to struggling communities. None of this would have been possible without the efforts of Daniel Hale Williams, the son of a barber, who made the courageous decision to dedicate his life to benefit humanity.

Discussion

Dr. Williams took it upon himself to make healthcare less segregated. Things continue to improve for minorities but do you think the U.S. will ever achieve equality for all of its citizens? Why or why not?

Arno Penzias and Robert Wilson cleaning the inside of the Holmdel Horn Antenna.

CHAPTER 9

The Answer Appeared as a Problem

- Arno Penzias & Robert Wilson

1964 was the year that humans first recognized evidence of the creation of space, the big bang. Until then, many had speculated about the birth of the universe, but that year, we actually saw evidence of the fireball that started it all. Discovering evidence of the big bang was an amazing twentieth-century leap forward in cosmological understanding. It came, almost without notice, to Arno Penzias and Robert Wilson, who were doing research at Bell Laboratories in New Jersey.

Penzias and Wilson were radio astronomers who set out to take measurements of radio outputs coming from the Cassiopeia constellation. To astronomers, "radio outputs" means some kind of electromagnetic, or EM, waves. EM waves include light and invisible waves such as X-rays, radio waves and microwaves.

When you see visible light coming from a star, chances are that the star is emitting other kinds of EM waves as well.

The Cassiopeia constellation appears in the northern sky during the winter time. This group of five stars was named by the ancient Greeks who thought that they resembled the vain Queen Cassiopeia seated on her throne. Modern children can recognize this group of stars. They call them the "Winter W" because when the stars of Cassiopeia are connected, the imaginary line linking them looks like the letter W.

The facility where Penzias and Wilson worked had a huge antenna called the Holmdel Horn Antenna. It was designed as part of an early satellite communication system. When someone on the other side of the world broadcasted a radio signal, the signal would hit an orbiting satellite. From there, the radio wave would bounce off the satellite to the Bell Labs antenna in New Jersey. In this way, even though radio waves move in a straight line, you could communicate with someone on the other side of Earth.

The Holmdel Horn Antenna looked nothing like antennas you might be familiar with. It was a 50-foot-long massive structure built in the middle of a field and was about five times as tall as Penzias and Wilson standing next to it. It was shaped a bit

Penzias and Wilson are shown here standing on the base of the Holmdel Horn Antenna. Their small office is also visible at the top of the stairs. The base of the gigantic structure can turn and the wheel can move the opening of the antenna. (Photograph courtesy of NASA.)

like a gigantic, squared-off, upward-curved trumpet. Built on a base that could rotate, it had a motorized wheel that allowed the horn to be pointed straight up or to the right or left. These two movable aspects made it possible for the horn to be pointed toward any area of the sky.

Also built onto the base of the Holmdel Antenna was a staircase leading to a small shed-like building at the mouthpiece of the trumpet-shaped structure. It was in this small metal control room with only two windows and a double door, that Penzias and Wilson worked. EM waves collected by the horn would be focused toward the control room where they would be amplified and converted into electric signals that would cause a pen on a chart recorder to move. The EM waves could not be seen or heard but they could be detected and recorded on paper. The scientists could read and analyze the lines drawn on the chart recorder.

Bell Labs had hired the two radio astronomers to use the Holmdel Horn communications antenna to do research. All Penzias and Wilson had to do was direct the antenna somewhere other than a satellite, and they could study radio waves received from outer space. You have to admit, that's a pretty cool idea.

Radio waves coming from the area of the Cassiopeia constellation were discovered some time before Penzias and Wilson, but no one had ever studied them as closely as these two men planned to do.

Before they pointed the antenna toward Cassiopeia to collect radio waves, they decided to check their equipment. To do this, they aimed the antenna toward an area without any apparent source of EM waves. The men were aware of several local radio wave sources that would be detected by the antenna. They reasoned that once they accounted for all of the known waves that appeared on their chart, like local TV and radio broadcasts, no signal should remain. If no additional waves were detected, their equipment was working properly.

They checked their antenna as planned. They pointed it toward empty space and removed the known waves. Then, expecting to see no other recorded signals, they found that they were left with a tiny signal on their chart recorder, an annoying signal similar to a hissing sound, that could not be explained.

The astronomers asked their colleagues to determine whether they had missed a local signal that needed to be removed. Everyone agreed that the men had followed the correct procedures. The antenna was pointing toward nothing, so no signal should remain. Penzias and Wilson were a little confused, but they were not ready to give up.

Because the hiss could not be explained, the next thing they needed to do was to find where the error was coming from. In 1964, because there was no computer or software to be checked, this was not complicated. They checked the connections and made sure all of the contacts were clean. They also tested the mechanical equipment, making sure that things moved the way they were supposed to. But the hiss was still there. It was like a puzzle. The two men anxiously tested everything they could think of, trying to find the source of the radio hiss.

Penzias and Wilson had to clean up a pigeon-caused mess in their antenna.

Running out of ideas, they took a closer look at the antenna itself. Wilson and Penzias were surprised to see that birds had nested in the antenna. "Of course," they laughed, "after all that work, this simple thing could be the source of our hiss!"

They carefully relocated the birds' nests from the antenna. Then, with soapy brushes in hand, they scrubbed out the residual bird poop. The massive antenna was restored to spick-and-span condition before they tried it again. But nope – the hiss was still there!

Meanwhile, about 25 miles away at Princeton University, an Ivy League research school, founded before the American Revolution, some students along with their physics professor, Robert Dicke, were struggling with a problem of their own.

At that time, Professor Dicke's students, like everyone else in America, were still reeling from the assassination of young

President John F. Kennedy less than a year before. They were also enjoying their youth, listening to music made by four long-haired boys who recently visited from Liverpool, England: the Beatles. And in Professor Dicke's class, these students were learning about the big bang.

The big bang theory states that fourteen billion years ago, all the matter in the entire universe was in a single point called the singularity. Then, for some reason that we still don't know, the singularity exploded, hurling material in all directions. The blast caused space to expand at speeds faster than we can imagine. According to the theory, this expansion is still going on today.

Professor Dicke and his students were doing some mathematical calculations about the big bang. They reasoned that if the universe began as visible glowing light that expanded and cooled, and this light was still expanding and cooling, scientists should be able to detect the leftover EM wave signal. They calculated that the signature of the big bang would appear as low-level waves, a cosmic microwave background (CMB), that could be noticed throughout the universe.

The thought of being able to detect the cosmic microwave background was a very exciting idea. The problem was that Dicke, the students, and the Princeton Physics Department had to figure out how to build equipment that could read waves from outer space. They thought about modifications they could make to a standard radio antenna. They wondered if an army surplus

store would have some kind of antenna left over from World War II. They even researched what it would take to build an antenna.

Back at Bell Labs, Penzias and Wilson were still seeing the signal on their chart after all they had done. They wondered if it was possible that they were simply looking in the wrong place. Even when they turned the antenna elsewhere, the hiss persisted. They pointed their antenna to lots of areas in the universe and that pesky hiss was always there!

Current (2013) photo of the Cosmic Microwave Background (CMB) Radiation in the universe, initially discovered by Penzias and Wilson. Image Courtesy of ESA/Planck.

Scratching their heads, exhausted of all ideas, they called a physics professor at Princeton who was teaching a class on radio waves. The call came to Dicke as he and other members of the Princeton Physics Department were in the process of building a 20-foot-tall antenna to be installed on the roof of the physics building.

Penzias and Willson described the hiss to Professor Dicke and asked if any of his students would be willing to try to figure out what was wrong with their equipment. Professor Dicke took notes as the Bell Lab scientists described the hiss to him. It was immediately obvious to Dicke what could cause the hiss, and he told Penzias and Wilson that he and his students would be in touch.

After sharing the news with his students, the professor drove over with them to Bell Labs to see for themselves. They all climbed the stairs of the Holmdel Antenna, crowding the little control room. The Princeton group couldn't believe what they were looking at. Penzias and Wilson had discovered the cosmic microwave background. The printout of the CMB hiss looked exactly as the Princeton students calculated it would!

Both groups — Penzias and Wilson from Bell Laboratories, and Professor Dicke and the Princeton Physics Department — published articles in the same volume of *Astrophysical Journal Letters*. The radio astronomers from Bell Labs wrote an article describing what they found. The article submitted by the Princeton group explained the findings. It was a year after the hiss was originally detected that the two groups announced the existence of CMB that had never been seen before.

The cosmic microwave background radiation discovered that day is what remains of the vanishing brilliance of the early universe. It had been whispering secrets into the Holmdel Antenna and other antennas unnoticed for decades. Since its discovery, scientists all over the world have been observing and

This Swedish postage stamp commemorates the discovery of CMB Radiation by Penzias and Wilson.

measuring it. Using CMB measurements, we now know that the shape of the universe is fairly flat. CMB measurements have also revealed that the background is not the same everywhere, a fact that could provide information about the formation of the universe. Now that humans are aware of the whisper from billions of years ago, there doesn't seem to be any limit to the secrets it will tell.

Discussion

Penzias and Wilson discovered evidence of the big bang. Do you think exploring the creation of the universe is anti-religious?

An illustration of how Henrietta Swan Leavitt studied photographic plates placed on a lightbox.

CHAPTER 10

Mapping the Cosmos

- Henrietta Swan Leavitt

Henrietta Swan Leavitt wasn't always deaf, but she was always smart. She grew up in Lancaster, Massachusetts during the 1870s. Even as a child, Leavitt took life seriously, a trait inherited from her Puritan ancestors who had settled in the area. Her serious side kept her dedicated to her family and church, but she was also a dreamer. From the front porch of her white clapboard house in the New England countryside, she would marvel at the multitude of stars that sprinkled the heavens. Leavitt wished she could tell by looking at them whether the stars were far away and huge, or close by and smaller. She had no idea that one day her curiosity would answer this question and allow scientists to unlock the secrets of the universe.

Having some wealth, and a great brain, the hardworking Leavitt was able to attend Oberlin College and Harvard University's school for women. She graduated with a bachelor's degree in 1892 and began working as a "computer" in the Harvard College Observatory. This was 50 years before the electronic computer's invention, when "computer" was a job title given to women who could compute quickly and accurately.

Shortly after taking the job, Leavitt travelled to Beloit, Wisconsin, where her father lived. While there, she became ill and began to lose her hearing. This illness and the progressive loss of her hearing would trouble her throughout her life, but neither sickness nor deafness would distract her from her work or her love for the stars.

While suffering in Beloit, Leavitt wrote to her boss back in the observatory. In her letters, she expressed disappointment about being away from the job that brought her such delight and pleasure. She even asked her boss to send her some work while she was recuperating.

Although she loved the stars, Leavitt's college studies included only one astronomy class. In that class, she learned that astronomers had partly solved the problem of determining how far away the stars were by using parallax. She also learned that parallax only worked for the closest stars.

Your eyes use parallax to tell how far away something is. To see this in action, close one eye and hold your finger out-

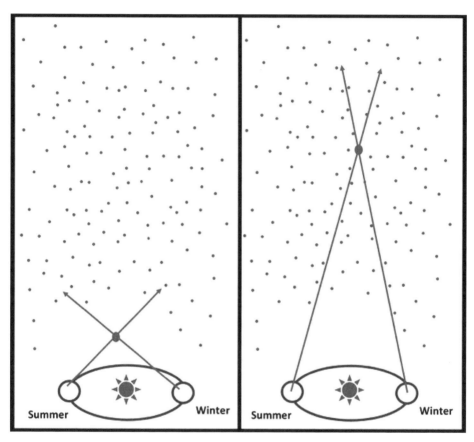

When viewing a close star from two separate Earth locations, the stars in the background are quite different. A star that is farther away will have more similar background stars. This difference is used to calculate the distant location of stars. However, this parallax system is limited because many stars are so far away that the background always looks the same.

stretched in front of you. Then switch eyes and notice how far your finger seems to jump. Now put your finger closer to your face, close one eye and then the other, and you will see that it jumps even more. Closer objects seem to move more than those farther away. Your brain calculates input from each eye to let you know whether something is near or far.

Viewing stars at different times is similar to looking with one eye and then the other. When you see a star from Earth's winter location and then you look at that same star in the summer, it will appear differently. Viewing the star from the winter location is like looking at it with one eye, and looking from the summer location is like using the other eye. If the star seems to have moved a lot between winter and summer, it is closer than stars that move less.

But parallax only works for a small fraction of stars. Most are so far away that they don't appear to move at all. What was needed was another way to measure the distance of stars that are farther away.

Mapping these faraway stars and observing their brightness was another responsibility Leavitt had at the observatory. She would examine photographic plates and record the brightness of stars that were found throughout the sky. These glass plates contained images that were taken using astrographs, which are telescopes that take pictures.

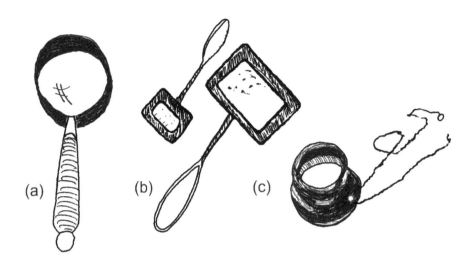

Some of Leavitt's tools used for measuring the brightness of stars. (a) A hand-held magnifying glass. (b) Fly spankers with markings to match images. (c) A magnifying eyepiece that could be worn around the neck when not in use. The light table she used is pictured in the illustration of Henrietta.

Leavitt used some unique tools to examine the photographic plates. She would place the plate to be studied onto a light box to observe the images. Her light box did not have a bulb inside of it because although the lightbulb had been invented, electricity was not yet in common use. Her lightbox was a slanted frame with a mirror underneath it to catch the light. To help her see the tiny dots of stars, Leavitt would sometimes use a hand-held magnifying glass or a magnifying eyepiece that she wore on a chain around her neck when she wasn't using it. The tools she used to measure the star size and brightness looked like tiny flyswatters. Leavitt called them "fly-spankers." A fly-spanker was a small piece of flat glass placed on a long handle. On the glass were markings that Leavitt would compare to the star images on the photographic plate.

The young woman was happy and proud to be doing this job. It was something most women could not do in the late 1800s. And although she would have been happy to do it for free, she was paid 30 cents per hour. That doesn't sound like much today, but back then it was as much money as a man would earn working in factories.

Some images Leavitt studied were taken at an observatory located near Lima, Peru. From her desk at Harvard, she documented the brightness of the shiny, white clouds that the explorer Ferdinand Magellan used to help him navigate as he made the first-ever trip around the globe. She was aware that she was one of very few people in Massachusetts who could recognize the Magellanic Clouds, which are only visible in the southern hemisphere.

Day after day, Leavitt pored over hundreds of pictures, each a blizzard of dots. She would locate a star on one image and compare it to another image of that same star on different nights. She did this because in addition to recording each star's brightness, Leavitt was also looking for special "variable" stars that go through a cycle from dim to bright and back again. This is different from the twinkling effect of stars, which is actually caused by Earth's atmosphere.

Leavitt had to look at the same stars over and over again in order to determine which were variables. This tedious task gave her mind time to wander, to dream about the size of the universe and the tremendous span between stars. As she recorded their brightness, she treated each star individually, often adding descriptive comments. She wished that there was a way their brightness could tell her how far away they were.

By 1908, Leavitt had recorded the brightness of tens of thousands of stars and identified 1,777 variables whose appearance changed. Later, a friend who worked with her described Leavitt as "a fiend for variable stars" and The Washington Post wrote that Leavitt was better at finding stars than any "theatrical producer." In her catalog of variable stars, she also noted that brighter variable stars seemed to change at a slower rate.

With permission from her boss, Leavitt looked into whether what she noticed was true. She focused her attention on 25 variable stars in the Small Magellanic Cloud that were too far away for parallax to work. There were two reasons why Leavitt chose these stars. The first was a practical one: all of them could be studied using photos from one astrograph. This would save money and it would ensure that the images didn't vary from one astrograph to another. The second reason was because they were in the same group, and therefore probably all a similar distance

from Earth. This would get rid of the problem of not knowing whether each star was small and close or big and far. The star that looked brighter than the rest would certainly be bigger than the rest.

For four years, Leavitt painstakingly graphed the brightness and the periods of her 25 chosen variable stars. She would

All of the stars in the Small Magellanic Cloud are approximately the same distance from us. Leavitt used this fact, combined with what we knew about the changing brightness of variable stars, to determine how far away this group was from Earth.

measure a dot as it swelled and weakened, writing tiny numbers on the glass. This task required much patience because a very bright variable might take months to go from bright to dim and then back to bright. The cycle of those that were not as bright might only take a few days. She persisted because she knew that if her assumption turned out to be true, her meticulous efforts would be worth the trouble.

As she plotted each star's brightness and period on her graph, she became more and more excited because with each point it became clearer that her observation might be true. She was thrilled when she placed the last data points and realized that there was a perfect relationship between brightness and cycle times seen in the variable stars. Her hard work and dedication had paid off! This was the key to unlocking the secrets of the universe and she knew it! The question she had asked as a child was about to be answered.

Her boss, Edward Pickering, was well aware of the value of Leavitt's discovery and the fact that women could not author scientific papers at that time. He could have easily taken credit for her work, but he was a fair and honest man. He released a paper, noting in the first sentence, "The following statement regarding the periods of 25 variable stars in the Small Magellanic Cloud has been prepared by Miss Leavitt."

In the paper, Leavitt provided what some have called a "standard candle" to measure the distance of faraway stars. She called for astronomers to use parallax to measure the distances of nearby variable stars that have the same cycle times as those she studied. Astronomers recognized that by doing this, the close stars would reveal the "actual brightness" of Leavitt's stars. Once the actual brightness was known, a faraway star's distance could be calculated.

Leavitt lived long enough to see her technique used to reveal that the Small Magellanic Cloud was nearly 200,000 light years from Earth – that's over a billion times of a billion miles! (1.2 quintillion miles; 2 quintillion kilometers)

To say that after her death Leavitt's technique continued to be used is an understatement. Her technique launched an entirely new understanding of the universe. Before her findings, astronomers believed that the universe was limited to the Milky Way Galaxy. They thought that faraway galaxies were merely dust clouds within the Milky Way. But, thanks to Leavitt, they realized the existence of thousands of galaxies much like the Milky Way. The great astronomer Harlow Shapley used Leavitt's technique to estimate the size of the Milky Way Galaxy and the sun's position within it. Edwin Hubble also used her technique to determine that the universe is expanding, a theory known as the big bang.

Using Leavitt's method, we can now measure the location of distant stars far beyond what could be achieved using parallax. Her technique makes it possible to measure incredible distances up to 20 million light years – the distance light could travel in 20 million years!

Henrietta Swan Leavitt was an unassuming, deaf woman troubled by illness throughout much of her life. But her insightful discovery changed the way we see the universe and all the heavenly bodies in it. Thinking beyond the mundane task she was assigned, Leavitt was able to provide an essential key to understanding our mysterious universe. It was an idea that went far beyond the dreams of a little girl sitting on her porch in New England more than 100 years ago.

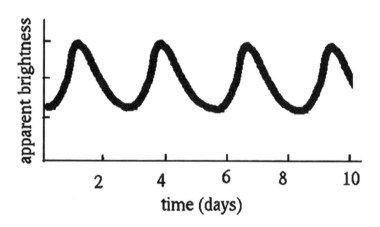

This is a graph of how the Cepheid variable stars that Leavitt was studying got bright and dim over time. Image Courtesy of NASA.

Discussion

In the early 1900s, few people hired woman as scientists. Pickering did but he paid them less than male scientists. Was he taking advantage of these women or helping them? Support your reasoning.

Additional Information and Further Reading

EARTH SCIENCE DISCOVERIES

Chapter 1 – Solving a Mystery with His Father

- The distinction between meteors and asteroids varies depending on what you read. At one point in time, anything that blazed across the sky was referred to as a meteor. The word asteroid refers to rocky bodies normally orbiting in the asteroid belt (between Mars and Jupiter). An asteroid knocked out of orbit and into Earth's atmosphere would cause a burning streak across the sky, so in older texts it would be called a meteor. Today, we know it was a dislodged asteroid that caused the extinction of the dinosaurs.

- Walter's father, Luis Walter Alvarez, won the Nobel Prize for Physics in 1968 for developing an improved bubble chamber that allowed him and his team to discover sub-atomic particles.

- Walter made the trip to Gubbio several times with his colleague, Bill Lowrie, a Scottish geologist.

- The pink limestone at Gubbio is unique. Limestone is a sedimentary rock, the kind of rock that forms layers and often contains fossils. But, the pink in this rock was caused by iron particles. These particles showed magnetic features that are not normally seen in sedimentary rock; they are usually only found in igneous rocks created from lava.

- At one time, the K-Pg boundary was called the K-T boundary. After it was determined that life changed there, the word Tertiary in the name (which simply means third) was changed to the more appropriate Paleogene (which refers to old life forms). Older texts will still refer to the K-T boundary, but the K-Pg boundary and K-T boundary are the same iridium-filled layer.

- The Chicxalube crater is 200,000 meters across and Meteor Crater in Arizona is 1,200 meters.

Further Reading:

T. Rex and the Crater of Doom was written by Walter Alvarez himself. He tells the story of his adventures in Gubbio. Most of this very interesting book is about the hunt for the crater and the struggles to convince the scientific community of the validity of their conclusion.

Chapter 2 - It Didn't Seem Possible

- Wegener called his idea "Continental Drift." The idea of moving continents is now called plate tectonics because huge plates of Earth on top of the liquid mantle cause the continents to move.

- The Mid-Atlantic Ridge, which separates Africa from South America, is part of the longest mountain range in the world. Most of it runs under the Atlantic Ocean, from Greenland to Bouvet Island, near Antarctica.

- Iceland was created exclusively by volcanoes of the mid-Atlantic.

- Up until about 170 million years ago, animals could walk from South America to Africa.

- In addition to the age of the Atlantic's floor, *Glomar Challenger* also discovered magnetic reversals in the volcanic rock under the ocean. These showed that the magnetic poles switch from north to south periodically. (This magnetic activity is what Walter Alvarez was studying in Gubbio's pink limestone.)

Further Reading:

Alfred Wegener: Creator of the Continental Drift Theory, written by Lisa Yount as part of the Makers of Modern Science Series, tells of Wegener's varied expeditions to Greenland as well as his Continental Drift theory.

CHEMISTRY DISCOVERIES
Chapter 3 - Averting a Disaster

- Mario Molina (Mexico), Sherwood Rowland (U.S.A.), and Paul Crutzen (Dutch, Netherlands) shared the 1995 Nobel Prize in Chemistry for their role in discovering the CFC threat to the ozone layer.

- Molina's full name is Mario José Molina-Pasqual Henriquez.
- Mario Molina was the first Mexican-born scientist to receive a Nobel Prize.
- Ozone is made of three oxygen atoms bound together. Normal oxygen that we breathe has two oxygen atoms. CFCs break the bond between oxygen atoms, turning ozone into regular breathing oxygen that provides no protection.
- The UV light that is so dangerous to us is actually what causes regular oxygen to bond and become ozone. The UV sunlight is what created Earth's ozone layer in the first place. That's why UV light is able to repair the ozone layer now that CFCs are no longer being added to the atmosphere.
- Cold conditions at the poles cause more damage to the ozone there.
- The Montreal Protocol that called for banning CFCs worldwide went into effect in 1989. It has been signed by all of the United Nation countries.
- President Obama awarded Mario Molina the Presidential Medal of Freedom in 2013.

Further Reading:

Mario Molina (Hispanic-American Biographies) written by Cynthia Guidici provides a good look at the life of this incredible man. It also has images of the ozone hole over Antarctica.

Chapter 4 - An Ancient Chinese Remedy Gets New Life

- Tu's full name is Tu Youyou. Tu is her family name and Youyou is her first name. This order is the opposite of the way names are treated in the West, where an individual's name comes first and their family name second.

- When Tu was asked to research ancient remedies, other scientists approached the malaria problem in several different ways. Some attempted to find a vaccine and others focused on controlling the mosquito population.

- The formula for Artemisinin is $C_{15}H_{22}O_5$ which means that there are 15 atoms of carbon, 22 atoms of hydrogen, and 5 atoms of oxygen in the molecule.

- When Tu Youyou went away to serve her country, she left her husband TingZhao and two daughters behind. Li Min was four years old, and Li Jun was only one.

- Tu's original research partner was Yu Yagang who studied mineral and animal substances, while Tu considered plants. The three scientists who were assigned to the project later were: Lang Linfu, Liu Jufu, and Zhong Yurong.

- Tu Youyou was educated at Peking University by Lin Qishou and Lou Zhicen. Lin taught her how to identify plants and Lou taught her extraction processes that are far more elaborate than simply brewing tea.

Further Reading:

To learn more, read *Tu Youyou's Journey in the Search for Artemisinin*, written by Wenhu Zhang, Yiran Shao, Dan Li, and Manyuan Wang. This is the most comprehensive book about Tu's experiences.

Chapter 5 - Purely by Accident

- Becquerel's father and his grandfather held similar positions to his. The phosphorescent materials collected by his grandfather were passed down to Henri from his father who had inherited them from his father.

- Henri Becquerel had one son, Jean who also grew up to be a physicist, making him the fourth generation of scientists in the Becquerel family.

- Marie and Pierre Curie determined that radioactivity was what Becquerel saw. Marie renamed Becquerel's rays "radioactivity."

- There are four types of radioactivity (alpha, beta, gamma, and neutrons). Becquerel detected two because uranium emits alpha and beta particles.

- Many types of radiation convert one element into another.

Further Reading:

The Nobel Prize.org site has biographical information on all who have been awarded this prestigious prize. It is recommended for Becquerel because there are few English books about him. He is mentioned in almost all texts about Marie Curie. For further reading, see https://www.nobelprize.org/prizes/physics/1903/becquerel/biographical/

MEDICAL DISCOVERIES

Chapter 6 - How One Nurse Saved Millions of Lives

- During the Crimean War, four times as many soldiers died from disease than battle injuries (80%). In the American Civil War this improved to about 62% dying from disease. To a large degree this is because of what we learned in Crimea.

- Thomas Edison recorded Florence Nightingale's voice in 1890. The recording can be heard online.

- International Nurses Day is celebrated around the world on the 12th of May, Florence Nightingale's birthday.

- During the Crimean War, Nightingale contracted an infection known as Crimean fever. She struggled with the illness for the rest of her life.

- Nightingale spoke English, French, Italian, and German

fluently. She learned mathematics, philosophy, Shakespearean literature, Latin, and Greek from her father.

- Florence was named after her birthplace: Florence, Italy.

- In 1855, Queen Victoria awarded Nightingale with an elaborate, jeweled pin bearing the words, "To Miss Florence Nightingale, as a mark of esteem and gratitude for her devotion towards the Queen's brave soldiers."

- The Crimean War ended March 30, 1856 with the signing of the Treaty of Paris in which Russia accepted defeat against Britain, France and the Ottoman Empire.

- The Lady with the Lamp is also sometimes referred to as the Angel of Crimea.

Further Reading:

There are two excellent, but very different, books about Florence Nightingale. *Florence Nightingale's Theology: Essays, Letters and Journal Notes* is a collection of the lady's own notes that were compiled in 2002 by Lynn McDonald. Florence's own writings tell the reader about the spirituality that drove her to action. The second book is more generally about her life and accomplishments, *Florence Nightingale: The Courageous Life of the Legendary Nurse* by K. Reef.

Chapter 7 - They Struck a Deal

- The American Fur Company (AFC) was founded in 1808, by John Jacob Astor, a German immigrant to the United States. During the 18th century, furs had become a major commodity in Europe and Asia. North America became a major supplier.

- The AFC Store is now the Beaumont Museum.

- During the ten years that Alexis spent with Dr. Beaumont, he travelled home to Canada a few times.

- Alexis St. Martin's exact age is unknown. Beaumont estimated that he was 20 at the time of the incident but some records suggest that he may have been up to ten years older.

- In addition to featuring horses and a cool fort, Mackinac Island is also currently famous for its fudge, art fairs, ghost stories, and bicycle riding

- The Grand Hotel on the island was built in 1887 as a resort for wealthy Chicagoans trying to escape the summer heat.

- The entire island of Mackinac is less than four square miles.

- Mackinac is in the state of Michigan between the upper and lower peninsula. It's in the water just at the tip of the "mitten" of the lower peninsula.

- The film *Somewhere in Time,* starring Christopher Reeves, was filmed on Mackinac Island.

- The fort is now a museum where guides dress as 1880s U.S. soldiers and civilians. While in uniform, they demonstrate how to use a musket, the type of smokey shotgun that wounded Alexis St. Martin.

Further reading:

In Dr. Beaumont's book, *Experiments and Observations on the Gastric Juice, and the Physiology of Digestion,* the doctor recalls the entire story of his experiences with Alexis St. Martin. The book is not as difficult to read as the title might lead you to believe.

Chapter 8 - The Barber's Son

- Daniel Hale Williams married Alice Johnson, whom he met in Washington D.C.

- Williams made trips to Nashville, Tennessee because he was a voluntary visiting clinical professor at Meharry Medical College.

- Williams became the first African-American charter member of the American College of Surgeons in 1913.

- Along with others, Williams is honored in the song *Black Man* by Stevie Wonder.

- First Lady Michelle Obama was born at Provident Hospital in 1964.

- Dr. Williams did not give his heart surgery patient any blood because before 1901 this was dangerous. In 1901,

Karl Landsteiner, an Austrian discovered the first human blood groups. And, it wasn't until 1941, that a black doctor, Charles Drew, developed ways to process and store blood.

Further Reading:

There are many children's books about Daniel Hale Williams. *Sure Hands Strong Heart – the Life of Daniel Hale Williams* written by Lillie Patterson is for a more mature reader. It covers his life and achievements in detail. There are also many books about famous African-Americans that include a section about Daniel Hale Williams.

ASTRONOMY DISCOVERIES
Chapter 9 - The Solution Disguised as a Problem

- A Belgian priest named Georges Lemaître was the first to suggest the big bang theory. He hypothesized that the universe began from a single atom. The use of the words "big bang" to describe the idea came from Fred Hoyle, a physicist, who was bashing the theory on BBC radio. Edwin Hubble normally gets credit for the idea but his publication came a little later in a much bigger journal. Lemaitre used Einstein's Relativity to predict the big bang.

- Hubble determined that the universe is expanding by using the Doppler Effect to show that galaxies are moving away. The colors of stars are shifting toward red, and their wavelengths are getting longer, which means they are moving away. The Doppler Effect in sound waves is more familiar to us. We can hear it when race cars or trains move away from us; their soundwaves get longer; their pitch decreases. In one the color moves down the rainbow; in the other, sound moves down the scale.

- The Holmdel Horn Antenna was originally part of the Echo Project wherein radio waves were bounced off of high-altitude metallic balloons (before satellites).

Further Reading:

Blind Watchers of the Sky: The People and Ideas that Shaped Our View of the Universe by Rocky Kolb tells the Penzias and Wilson story by following a photon's journey toward New Jersey. It tells a delightful story of astronomy, from ancient to modern times.

Chapter 10 - Another Step in the Cosmic Ladder

- The glass plates observed by Leavitt were reverse images. The stars appeared as black dots on clear glass (similar to Becquerel's plates).

- A light year is a measurement of distance. It is how far light, which seems to move infinitely fast, can travel in a year. Think about that. It's unbelievably far.

- Harvard's Women's School from which Leavitt graduated, later became Radcliffe.

- Henrietta Leavitt was a member of the American Association of University Women.

- The "variable" stars Leavitt studied are officially called Cepheid Variables.

- To calculate the distance of a star once the star's actual brightness is known, astronomers use the Inverse Square Law. A star that is 4 times dimmer than another must be 2 times as far away. (Newton's Law of Gravity which explains gravity between two objects separated by distance, and Coulomb's Law which describes the effect of electromagnetic charges over distance, are also Inverse Square Laws.)

- Leavitt's mother's name was also Henrietta Swan (maiden name Kendrick). Her father, Rev. George Roswell Leavitt was the pastor of Pilgrim Congregational Church. Henrietta was the oldest of seven children. Her siblings were: Martha, George, Caroline, Mira (died at 2 years old), Roswell (died at 15 months), and Darwin.

- The three steps in the Cosmic Ladder that astronomers use to measure distances of farther and farther stars are (1) parallax,

(2) Leavitt's Law, and (3) Supernovae. Parallax is looking at the same thing from different perspectives. Leavitt's Law, of course, found a correlation between a variable star's brightness and its period. Supernovae is a similar correlation – how long you are able to see the explosion of a supernova is related to how far away it is.

Further Reading:

Miss Leavitt's Stars: The Untold Story of the Woman Who Discovered How to Measure the Universe written by George Johnson, an award-winning science reporter. This book is literature. The story tells all that is known about Henrietta. It explains the science beautifully and goes on to give details of many scientists who used Leavitt's Law to reveal secrets of the universe.

Acknowledgements

I'd like to thank my husband for providing technical assistance, and my entire family for supporting my book quest. I would also like to thank the local SCBWI group and the Geneva Night Writers for their help and encouragement. Many thanks to Sheri Tan for her editing skills and Barb Barrows for her knowledge. And, I would like to thank Ruth Wan, Daniele Lee and the entire World Scientific staff for making my dream of becoming an author a reality.

About the Author

Diane Lincoln is a former high school and middle school science teacher with two decades of experience bringing fascinating science stories to life for her students. She holds a Doctorate in Education and has taught graduate-level courses in science education to other teachers wanting to hone their skills. Diane has won awards for her fictional stories and poetry in print media, and has published a book of poetry. *Science Discovery Files* is her first foray into the world of non-fiction science publishing. She is looking forward to sharing some of her many stories that breathe life into the exciting world of scientific discovery.